Healthy Cooking

Cookbook for beginners
Against cardiovascular disease
And for everyday dietary health

Sophia Concier

Contents

Introduction

Welcome to "Healthy Cooking for Beginners: Against Cardiovascular Diseases." This book is not just about food and cooking; it's about embracing a journey that can dramatically transform your life. It's about making choices that radiate love and respect for your body. It's about understanding how your heart — the incredible engine of your being — functions best when nurtured with  the right fuel. Finding the time and energy to focus on nutrition can be challenging in a constantly moving world. Quick, convenient food often wins out over meals that require time and preparation. However, with heart disease as a leading cause of death globally, it's clear that our eating habits can profoundly influence our health.

This alarming fact is precisely why "Healthy Cooking for Beginners: Against Cardiovascular Diseases" was conceived. We're on a mission to guide you down a path where heart health is not an abstract concept but a tangible result of everyday decisions. We believe in the immense power of our daily food choices and how they can fuel or fail our bodies.

This book is not a magic potion that promises immediate results. Instead, it's a tool, a reliable friend you can turn to when navigating the sometimes confusing landscape of nutrition. Our objective is to equip you with the knowledge and skills to cook delicious meals and fortify your heart.

Think about your body as a complex, bustling metropolis. The heart, much like city hall, keeps everything running smoothly. But to do so, it needs high-quality fuel — nutritious food that nourishes and supports its functions. Feeding it with low-grade fuel — processed, unhealthy foods — is only a matter of time before the engine falters.

But how do we ensure we provide our bodies with the proper fuel? That's where "Healthy Cooking for Beginners: Against Cardiovascular Diseases" comes in. We've curated a selection of recipes that use simple, wholesome, heart-friendly ingredients. They're easy to prepare, even for beginners, and you don't need a fully equipped gourmet kitchen or expensive, hard-to-find ingredients to make them.

Through these pages, you'll explore the world of nutritious fruits and vegetables, lean proteins, fiber-rich grains, and omega-3-packed seafood. You'll learn to cook delicious meals and understand and appreciate the nutritional science behind your food.

Eating well shouldn't mean breaking the bank, either. We've designed budget-friendly recipes without compromising taste or nutritional value. We've covered you, from breakfasts that kick-start your day to nourishing main meals to desserts that satisfy your sweet tooth without guilt.

In addition, we'll delve into meal planning and preparation — a game-changer for those with busy schedules. By planning and prepping, you can ensure you have heart-healthy meals ready when needed. This approach saves time, money, and stress and helps you avoid consuming unhealthy convenience foods.

This journey you're about to embark upon is an investment in yourself, a commitment to enhancing your health one delicious meal at a time. Embrace it with curiosity, enthusiasm, and self-compassion. Change doesn't happen overnight; every small step toward a healthier lifestyle counts.

"Healthy Cooking for Beginners: Against Cardiovascular Diseases" is not just a cookbook — it's a lifesaver. It represents a choice to prioritize your health, respect your body, and savor the pleasure of home-cooked, nutritious meals.

We hope this book inspires, guides you, and becomes a trusted companion in your kitchen. Let's make heart-healthy cooking a joy rather than a chore. Let's celebrate the art of cooking and the science of eating for a healthier heart.

So, please put on your apron, gather your ingredients, and let's embark on this culinary adventure together. We can't wait to see the healthier, happier you that emerges from this journey. Here's to taking the first step toward a heart-healthy future!

Enjoy your journey with "Healthy Cooking for Beginners: Against Cardiovascular Diseases"! Let's get cooking.

As you delve deeper into "Healthy Cooking for Beginners: Against Cardiovascular Diseases," you'll find that preparing nutritious meals is both a science and an art. You'll learn how various ingredients benefit your heart and how to combine them in ways that create meals that are as pleasing to the palate as they are beneficial to your health. It isn't a restrictive, tedious approach to eating—it's quite the opposite. As you discover the wide variety of flavors, textures, and aromas of heart-healthy foods, you'll find that eating well is a pleasure, not a punishment. We want to dispel the myth that healthy food is bland or unsatisfying. On the contrary, it can be a delight, a daily source of joy that keeps your heart in shape and brightens your life.

Alongside recipes, you'll also find handy tips and tricks to make your cooking journey smoother and more enjoyable. You'll learn how to store ingredients for optimal freshness, how to repurpose leftovers into delicious new meals, and how to make the most of your time in the kitchen. We understand that life is busy, and we're committed to making the path to heart health as efficient and straightforward as possible.

In crafting this book, we've drawn on the latest scientific research on nutrition and heart health. Still, we've also remembered the wisdom of generations past—people who understood intuitively that the key to a long, healthy life lay in natural, unprocessed foods. The recipes you'll find here are a marriage of science and tradition, blending the best of both worlds for your benefit.

Ultimately, "Healthy Cooking for Beginners: Against Cardiovascular Diseases" is more than a book—it's a manifesto for a lifestyle that prioritizes health without sacrificing pleasure. It's a call to take charge of your well-being and understand your immense power to shape your health outcomes.

Remember, every meal is an opportunity to nourish your body and heart. Every bite can be a step towards a healthier, more vibrant life. It's never too late to start making better food choices, and this book is here to guide you every step of the way.

So, are you ready to embrace this life-enhancing journey? Are you prepared to discover just how delicious heart-healthy cooking can be? If the answer is yes, then let's get started. Your heart is counting on you, and with "Healthy Cooking for Beginners: Against Cardiovascular Diseases" in your kitchen, you have everything you need to succeed. Let's celebrate good food and good health, one delicious, heart-nourishing meal at a time.

Chapter 1
Starting the Day Right - Breakfast Recipes

1. Berrylicious Oatmeal

Ingredients:
1/2 cup of oats (150 calories)
1 cup of water (0 calories)
1 cup of mixed berries (blueberries, strawberries, raspberries - around 70 calories)
One tablespoon of chia seeds (60 calories)
One tablespoon of honey (64 calories)

Preparation:
In a pot, bring the water to a boil. Add the oats and reduce the heat to medium. Cook for about 10 minutes or until the oats are your desired texture.
While the oats are cooking, rinse your mixed berries under cool water.
Once the oats are done, pour them into a bowl. Top with mixed berries, chia seeds, and a drizzle of honey.
Enjoy your heart-healthy, fiber-filled breakfast!
Total Calories: ~344

Please note that the calorie count can vary slightly depending on the exact amount and type of ingredients used. This oatmeal recipe is quick and easy to make. Still, also loaded with antioxidants from the berries, omega-3

fatty acids from the chia seeds, and a natural sweetener (honey) instead of processed sugar.
Now, let's move on to the second recipe:

2. Veggie-Loaded Scramble

Ingredients:
Two egg whites (34 calories)
1/2 cup of spinach (3 calories)
1/4 bell pepper (12 calories)
1/4 tomato (6 calories)
One slice of whole-grain bread (70 calories)
Salt and pepper to taste (negligible calories)
Instructions:
Heat a non-stick skillet over medium heat.
While the skillet is heating, chop the spinach, bell pepper, and tomato.
Add the egg whites to the skillet and start to scramble them.
Just before the eggs are fully cooked, add the spinach, bell pepper, and tomato. Continue to cook until the veggies are heated, and the eggs are fully cooked.
While the scramble is cooking, toast your bread.
Serve the scramble with the whole-grain toast on the side.
Enjoy this protein and fiber-packed breakfast!
Total Calories: ~125

3. Quinoa Breakfast Porridge

Ingredients:
1/2 cup of cooked quinoa (111 calories)
1 cup of almond milk (60 calories)

One ripe banana, sliced (105 calories)
One tablespoon of honey (64 calories)
A pinch of cinnamon (negligible calories)
Instructions:
In a pot, combine cooked quinoa and almond milk. Bring to a simmer over medium heat.
Stir occasionally and cook until it reaches a creamy consistency.
Stir in the honey and cinnamon.
Serve hot topped with banana slices.

Total Calories: ~340

4. Avocado Toast with Poached Egg

Ingredients:
One slice of whole-grain bread (70 calories)1/2 ripe avocado (120 calories)
One egg (72 calories)
Salt and pepper to taste (negligible calories)
Instructions:
Toast the bread until golden.
In the meantime, poach an egg by bringing a pot of water to a simmer, crack the egg into a cup, create a gentle whirlpool, and carefully tip the egg into the water. Cook for 4 minutes for a runny yolk or longer for a firmer yolk.
Spread the ripe avocado on the toasted bread and season with salt and pepper.
Carefully place the poached egg on top.

Enjoy right away.

Total Calories: ~262

5. Green Smoothie Bowl

Ingredients:
1 cup of spinach (7 calories)
One ripe banana (105 calories)
1/2 avocado (120 calories)
1 cup of almond milk (60 calories)
A handful of your favorite fruits for topping (calories will vary)
One tablespoon of honey (64 calories)
Instructions:
Combine the spinach, banana, avocado, and almond milk until smooth.
Pour into a bowl, and decorate with your favorite fruits on top.
Drizzle with honey for added sweetness.
Enjoy as a refreshing breakfast or snack.

Total Calories: ~356 (without additional fruit)

6. Chia Seed Pudding

Ingredients:
Two tablespoons of chia seeds (138 calories)
1 cup of almond milk (60 calories)
Your favorite fruits for topping (calories will vary)
A handful of nuts for topping (calories will go)
Instructions:

In a jar or glass, stir together chia seeds and almond milk. Let sit for a few minutes, then start again to prevent clumping.
Cover and refrigerate for at least 2 hours or overnight.
Top with your favorite fruits and nuts before eating.
Total Calories: ~198 (without additional fruit and nuts)

7. Hearty Breakfast Quinoa Salad

Ingredients:
1/2 cup of cooked quinoa (111 calories)
 1/4 cup of chopped veggies (calories will vary)
One boiled egg (78 calories)
A squeeze of lemon juice (4 calories)
Instructions:
In a bowl, combine the cooked quinoa and chopped veggies.
Squeeze some fresh lemon juice over the top for flavor.
Top with a boiled egg.
Enjoy as a filling, protein-packed breakfast.
Total Calories: ~193 (without additional veggies)

8. Overnight Oats with Berries and Nuts

Ingredients:
1/2 cup of oats (150 calories)
1/2 cup of Greek yogurt (75 calories)
3/4 cup of almond milk (45 calories)
One tablespoon of honey (64 calories)
A handful of fresh berries (calories will vary)
A sprinkle of your favorite nuts (calories will vary)

Instructions:

Combine oats, Greek yogurt, almond milk, and honey in a jar.

Cover and refrigerate overnight.

In the morning, top with fresh berries and a sprinkle of nuts.

Enjoy chilled.

Total Calories: ~334

(without additional berries and nuts)

9. Egg and Veggie Muffins

Ingredients:

Four egg whites (68 calories)

1/2 cup of mixed veggies (like bell peppers, onions, spinach - calories will vary)

Salt and pepper to taste (negligible calories)

Instructions:

Preheat your oven to 350 degrees Fahrenheit (175 degrees Celsius) and grease a muffin tin.

Add your favorite chopped veggies to the egg whites in a bowl.

Season with a bit of salt and pepper.

Pour the mixture into the muffin tin and bake for 20-25 minutes or until set.

Enjoy these protein-packed, veggie-filled muffins for a grab-and-go breakfast.

Total Calories: ~68 (without additional veggies)

10. Greek Yogurt Parfait

Ingredients:
1 cup of Greek yogurt (150 calories)
One tablespoon of honey (64 calories)
A handful of granola (calories will vary)
A handful of fresh berries (calories will change)

Instructions:
Layer Greek yogurt, honey, granola, and fresh berries in a glass or jar.
Repeat the layers until your glass is full.
Enjoy immediately for a crunchy, creamy, and sweet breakfast.

Total Calories: ~214 (without additional granola and berries)

11. Tropical Smoothie
Ingredients:
One ripe banana (105 calories)
1/2 cup of pineapple chunks (41 calories)
1 cup of spinach (7 calories)
1 cup of almond milk (60 calories)
Instructions:
Combine banana, pineapple chunks, spinach, and almond milk until smooth in a blender.
Pour into a glass and enjoy it as a refreshing breakfast or snack.

Total Calories: ~213

12. Banana Nut Oatmeal

Ingredients:
1/2 cup of oats (150 calories)
1 cup of water (0 calories)
One ripe banana, sliced (105 calories)
A sprinkle of your favorite nuts (calories will vary)
Preparation:
In a pot, bring the water to a boil. Add the oats and reduce
the heat to medium. Cook for about 10 minutes or until the oats are your desired texture.
Once the oats are done, pour them into a bowl. Top with the banana slices and a sprinkle of nuts.
Enjoy this heart-healthy, protein-packed breakfast.

Total Calories: ~255 (without additional nuts)

13. Apple Cinnamon Overnight Oats

Ingredients:
1/2 cup of oats (150 calories)
3/4 cup of almond milk (45 calories)
One apple chopped (52 calories)
A sprinkle of cinnamon (negligible calories)
Instructions:
Combine oats, almond milk, chopped apple, and cinnamon in a jar.
Cover and refrigerate overnight.
Enjoy chilled in the morning for a sweet, satisfying breakfast.

Total Calories: ~247

14. Fruit and Nut Granola Bars

Ingredients:

2 cups of oats (600 calories)

1 cup of mixed nuts, chopped (800 calories)

1/2 cup of honey (517 calories)

1 cup of dried fruit (calories will vary)

Preparation:

Preheat your oven to 350 degrees Fahrenheit (175 degrees Celsius) and line a baking pan with parchment paper. Combine oats, mixed nuts, honey, and dried fruit in a bowl.

Press the mixture into the prepared baking pan and bake for 20-25 minutes or until golden brown.

Let cool before cutting into bars.

These bars make a fantastic grab-and-go breakfast or snack.

Total Calories: ~1917 (without additional dried fruit; yields multiple servings)

15. Avocado and Tomato on Whole Wheat Toast

Ingredients:

One slice of whole wheat toast (80 calories)

1/2 ripe avocado (120 calories)

One small tomato, sliced (16 calories)

Salt and pepper to taste (negligible calories)

Instructions:

Toast the whole wheat bread until golden.

Spread the ripe avocado on the toasted bread.

Top with tomato slices and season with a bit of salt and pepper.

Enjoy right away for a fresh, flavorful breakfast.

Total Calories: ~216

16. Berry Smoothie

Ingredients:

1 cup of mixed berries (50 calories)

One ripe banana (105 calories)

1 cup of almond milk (60 calories)

Instructions:

Combine mixed berries, bananas, and almond milk until smooth.

Pour into a glass and enjoy it as a refreshing breakfast or snack.

Total Calories: ~215

17. Peanut Butter Banana

Toast

Ingredients:

One slice of whole-grain bread (70 calories)

One tablespoon of natural peanut butter (90 calories)

One banana, sliced (105 calories)

Instructions:

Toast the whole grain bread until golden.

Spread the peanut butter on the toasted bread.

Top with banana slices.

Enjoy right away for a protein-packed, energy-boosting breakfast.

Total Calories: ~265

18. Veggie Scramble

Ingredients:

Two egg whites (34 calories)

1/2 cup of mixed veggies (like bell peppers, onions, spinach - calories will vary)

Salt and pepper to taste (negligible calories)

Instructions:

In a non-stick skillet, sauté the mixed veggies until soft.

Whisk the egg whites in a bowl, then pour them over the veggies in the skillet.

Cook, stirring occasionally, until the eggs are set.

Season with a bit of salt and pepper.

Enjoy this healthy, veggie-packed scramble for breakfast.

Total Calories: ~34 (without additional veggies)

19. High-Protein Tofu Scramble

Ingredients:

1 cup of tofu, crumbled (188 calories)

1/2 cup of bell peppers, diced (23 calories)

1/2 cup of onions, chopped (30 calories)

Two tablespoons of nutritional yeast (60 calories)

Salt and pepper to taste (negligible calories)

Instructions:

Sauté bell peppers and onions until softened.

Add the crumbled tofu and cook for a few more minutes.

Stir in the nutritional yeast, salt, and pepper.

Serve hot for a hearty, protein-packed breakfast.

Total Calories: ~301

20. Greek Yogurt Parfait

Ingredients:

1 cup of Greek yogurt (150 calories)

1/2 cup of granola (209 calories)

1/2 cup of mixed berries (42 calories)

Instructions:

Layer Greek yogurt, granola, and mixed berries in a glass.

Repeat the layers until all ingredients are used.

Serve immediately or refrigerate overnight for a flavorful, satisfying breakfast.

Total Calories: ~401

21. Power Green Smoothie

Ingredients:

1 cup of spinach (7 calories)

One banana (105 calories)

1 cup of almond milk (60 calories)

One tablespoon of chia seeds (69 calories)

One tablespoon of almond butter (98 calories)

Instructions:

Combine all ingredients in a blender.

Blend until smooth.

Serve immediately for a nutrient-rich, energizing breakfast.

Total Calories: ~339

22. Egg and Avocado Breakfast Burrito

Ingredients:

One whole-grain tortilla (130 calories)
One egg scrambled (78 calories)
1/2 avocado, sliced (120 calories)
1/4 cup of black beans (55 calories)
Instructions:
Lay the tortilla flat and spread the scrambled egg in the middle.
Add the sliced avocado and black beans.
Roll up the tortilla, cut it in half, and serve for a well-rounded, delicious breakfast.

Total Calories: ~383

23. Quinoa Breakfast Bowl
Ingredients:
1 cup of cooked quinoa (222 calories)
1/2 cup of blueberries (42 calories)
1/4 cup of almonds, sliced (207 calories)
Drizzle of honey (64 calories)
Instructions:
Combine the cooked quinoa, blueberries, and slivered almonds in a bowl.
Drizzle with honey.
Serve immediately for a hearty, wholesome breakfast.

Total Calories: ~535

24. Peanut Butter Banana Smoothie
Ingredients:
One banana (105 calories)
One tablespoon of peanut butter (94 calories)

1 cup of almond milk (60 calories)
One tablespoon of flaxseeds (55 calories)
Instructions:
Combine all ingredients in a blender.
Blend until smooth.
Serve immediately for a protein-rich, filling breakfast.
Total Calories: ~314

25. Hearty Veggie and Egg Muffins

Ingredients:
Four eggs (312 calories)
1/2 cup of mixed veggies, diced (calories will vary)
1/4 cup of shredded cheese (110 calories)
Salt and pepper to taste (negligible calories)
Instructions:
Preheat your oven to 350°F (175°C) and grease a muffin tin.
Whisk the eggs in a bowl, season with salt and pepper.
Add the mixed veggies and cheese to the eggs and stir to combine.
Divide the mixture among the muffin cups and bake for 20-25 minutes or until the eggs are set.
Enjoy this high-protein, veggie-packed egg muffins for breakfast.

Total Calories: ~422 (without additional veggies)

Chapter 2
Energizing Midmorning Snacks

Midmorning is necessary to reinforce energy. It is my advice for your well-being. Fast and nutritious foods, in the correct dose and calories.

1. Apple Slices with Almond Butter
Ingredients:
One apple (95 calories)
Two tablespoons of almond butter (196 calories)

2. Greek Yogurt with Berries
Ingredients:
1 cup of Greek yogurt (150 calories)
1/2 cup of mixed berries (35 calories)

3. Celery Sticks with Hummus
Ingredients:
Two celery sticks (10 calories)
Two tablespoons of hummus (70 calories)

4. Banana and Almond Smoothie
Ingredients:
One banana (105 calories)
1 cup of almond milk (60 calories)

5. Handful of Mixed Nuts
Ingredients:

1/4 cup of mixed nuts (200 calories)

6. Cottage Cheese with Pineapple
Ingredients:
1/2 cup of cottage cheese (81 calories)
1/2 cup of diced pineapple (41 calories)

7. Carrot Sticks with Guacamole
Ingredients:
One medium carrot (25 calories)
2 tablespoons of guacamole (60 calories)

8. Sliced Pear with Walnuts
Ingredients:
1 pear (102 calories)
10 walnut halves (130 calories)

9. Rice Cake with Peanut Butter
Ingredients:
1 rice cake (35 calories)
1 tablespoon of peanut butter (94 calories)

10. Greek Yogurt with Honey and Almonds
Ingredients:
1/2 cup of Greek yogurt (75 calories)
1 tablespoon of honey (64 calories)
10 almonds (70 calories)

11. Boiled Egg with Cherry Tomatoes
Ingredients:
1 boiled egg (68 calories)
1 cup of cherry tomatoes (27 calories)

12. Grapes and Cheese Cubes
Ingredients:1 cup of grapes (104 calories)
1 oz of cheddar cheese (113 calories)

13. Mandarin Oranges with Pistachios
Ingredients:
2 mandarin oranges (80 calories)
1 oz of pistachios (158 calories)

14. Cucumber Slices with Tzatziki
Ingredients:
1/2 cucumber (23 calories)
2 tablespoons of tzatziki (30 calories)

15. Melon and Prosciutto
Ingredients:
1 cup of melon (60 calories)
1 oz of prosciutto (50 calories)

16. Cherry Smoothie
Ingredients:
1 cup of cherries (87 calories)
1/2 cup of almond milk (30 calories)

17. Popcorn and Dried Fruit
Ingredients:
1 cup of popcorn (31 calories)
1/4 cup of dried fruit (100 calories)

18. Mini Bell Peppers with Cream Cheese
Ingredients:
4 mini bell peppers (120 calories)
2 tablespoons of cream cheese (102 calories)

19. Frozen Blueberries and Greek Yogurt
Ingredients:
1/2 cup of frozen blueberries (40 calories)
1/2 cup of Greek yogurt (75 calories

20. Mango and Cottage Cheese
Ingredients:
1 cup of sliced mango (99 calories)
1/4 cup of cottage cheese (55 calories)

21. Almond Dates
Ingredients:
3 dates (200 calories)
6 almonds (42 calories)

22. Kiwi and Yogurt
Ingredients:
1 kiwi (61 calories)
1/2 cup of Greek yogurt (75 calories)

23. Chia Pudding
Ingredients:
2 tablespoons of chia seeds (138 calories)
1/2 cup of almond milk (30 calories)

24. Berry and Nut Yogurt
Ingredients:
1/2 cup of Greek yogurt (75 calories)
1/4 cup of mixed berries (21 calories)
1/4 cup of mixed nuts (200 calories)

25. Avocado and Tomato Salsa
Ingredients:

1/2 avocado (120 calories)
1/2 cup of tomato salsa (36 calories)

Chapter 3
Nourishing Midday Meals. Heart-Healthy Lunches for the Active Lifestyle

These recipes incorporate ingredients - lean white meats, a rainbow of vegetables, and the freshest fish - to offer you a spectrum of essential nutrients. They are straightforward to prepare, and the ingredients can be sourced without breaking the bank. The time required to whip up these meals is minimal, allowing you to enjoy a nutritious lunch even on your busiest days.
We want you to see these recipes not as a strict regime but as an inspiring starting point toward embracing a healthier lifestyle. Feel free to experiment, substitute, and create your versions. After all, the kitchen is the best playground for adults.
Embark on this culinary journey towards heart health with us, and let's make lunchtime a delightful and nutritious affair! Remember, the food you eat can be the safest or most potent medicine.

Recipes

1. Grilled Chicken Salad
Ingredients:
200g chicken breast (330 calories), 2 cups mixed salad greens (20 calories), 10 cherry tomatoes (30 calories), 1 cucumber (16 calories), 2 tablespoons olive oil (238

calories), 50g crumbled feta cheese (142 calories), and the juice of 1 lemon (12 calories). A pinch of salt (0 calories).

Preparation:
Season the chicken with salt, pepper, and lemon juice. Grill until fully cooked (about 15-20 minutes). Slice the cooked chicken and place over the mixed salad greens, cherry tomatoes, cucumber slices, and crumbled feta. Drizzle olive oil and additional lemon juice on top.
Time:
 25 minutes.
Estimated Cost:
 $7-$9.
Total: ~788 calories.

2. Turkey & Veggie Skewers
Ingredients:
200g turkey breast (440 calories), 300g mixed bell peppers (144 calories), juice of 1 lemon (12 calories), and 1g of salt (0 calories).
Preparation:
Alternate turkey and peppers on skewers, then grill, turning occasionally and drizzling with lemon juice and salt.

Time:
 15 minutes.
Estimated Cost:
Around $6-$8.
Total: ~596 calories.

3. Zesty Turkey Lettuce Wraps
Ingredients:
200g ground turkey (440 calories), 300g lettuce (45 calories), juice of 1 lemon (12 calories), 1g of salt (0 calories).
Preparation:
Cook turkey, scoop into lettuce leaves, and sprinkle with lemon juice and salt.
Time:
15 minutes.

Estimated Cost:
Around $6-$8.
Total: ~497 calories. It can be paired with a side dish.

4. Baked Chicken & Sweet Potato
Ingredients:
200g chicken breast (330 calories), 200g sweet potato (180 calories), 100g broccoli (55 calories), juice of 1 lemon (12 calories), and 1g of salt (0 calories).
Preparation:
Bake chicken, sweet potato, and broccoli together, then drizzle with lemon juice and sprinkle with salt.

Time:
15 minutes.
Estimated Cost:
Around $7-$9.
Total: ~577 calories.

5. Herb-Roasted Turkey and Quinoa Salad
Ingredients:
200g turkey breast (440 calories), 1 cup cooked quinoa (222 calories), juice of 1 lemon (12 calories), mixed herbs, 1g of salt (0 calories).
Preparation:
With mixed herbs. Serve with a side of cooked quinoa drizzled with lemon juice and salt.
Time:
15 minutes.
Estimated Cost:
Around $7-$9.
Total: ~674 calories.

6. Grilled Salmon and Green Beans
Ingredients:
200g salmon fillet (367 calories), 300g green beans (90 calories), juice of 1 lemon (12 calories), 1g of salt (0 calories).
Preparation:
Grill the salmon fillet and steam the green beans. Serve with a squeeze of lemon juice and a pinch of salt.
Time:
15 minutes.
Estimated Cost:
Around $8-$10.
Total: ~469 calories. It can be paired with a side dish.

7. Chicken Stir-Fry with Mixed Vegetables

Ingredients:

200g chicken breast (330 calories), 300g mixed vegetables (like bell peppers, carrots, and snow peas - approx. 150 calories), juice of 1 lemon (12 calories), and 1g of salt (0 calories).

Preparation:

Stir-fry chicken and mixed vegetables in a pan, then serve with lemon juice and salt drizzle.

Time:

15 minutes.

Estimated Cost

Around $6-$8.

Total: ~492 calories. It can be paired with a side dish.

.

8. Tilapia with Steamed Broccoli

Ingredients:

200g tilapia (296 calories), 300g broccoli (155 calories), juice of 1 lemon (12 calories), 1g of salt (0 calories).

Preparation:

Steam tilapia and broccoli, then sprinkle with lemon juice and salt.

Time:

15 minutes.

Estimated Cost:

Around $6-$8.

Total: ~463 calories. It can be paired with a side dish.

9. Tuna Salad with Whole Wheat Bread

Ingredients:

200g canned tuna in water (232 calories), 2 slices of whole wheat bread (200 calories), mixed greens (25 calories), juice of 1 lemon (12 calories), and 1g of salt (0 calories).
Preparation:
Mix tuna with greens, lemon juice, and salt. Serve on whole wheat bread.
Time:
 10 minutes.
Estimated Cost:
Around $4-$6.
Total: ~469 calories. It can be paired with a side dish.

10. Turkey and Red Cabbage Salad
Ingredients:
 200g turkey breast (440 calories), 200g red cabbage (88 calories), 100g canned tuna in water (116 calories), juice of 1 lemon (12 calories), and 1g of salt (0 calories).
Preparation:
Chop turkey and cabbage. Add drained tuna. Drizzle with lemon juice and sprinkle with salt.

Time:
10 minutes.
Estimated Cost:
Around $7-$10.
Total: ~656 calories.

11. Chicken with Broccoli and Carrots Stir Fry
Ingredients:

200g chicken breast (330 calories), 150g broccoli (51 calories), 150g carrots (62 calories), juice of 1 lemon (12 calories), and 1g of salt (0 calories).
Preparation:
Sauté chicken, broccoli, and carrots. Finish with lemon juice and salt.
Time:
15 minutes.
Estimated Cost:
Around $6-$8.
Total: ~455 calories. It can be paired with a side dish.

12. Chicken with Mixed Peppers Stir Fry
Ingredients:
200g chicken breast (330 calories), 150g red bell pepper (47 calories), 150g yellow bell pepper (50 calories), juice of 1 lemon (12 calories), and 1g of salt (0 calories).
Preparation:
Sauté chicken and mixed bell peppers. Finish with lemon juice and salt.

Time:
15 minutes.
Estimated Cost:
Around $6-$8.
Total: ~439 Calories.
It can be paired with a side dish.

13. Pan-Seared Salmon & Quinoa Salad
Ingredients:

200g salmon (416 calories), 150g cooked quinoa (208 calories), juice of 1 lemon (12 calories), 1g of salt (0 calories).
Preparation:
Pan-sear the salmon and serve it over a bed of cooked quinoa. Drizzle with lemon juice and salt.

Time: 12 minutes
Estimated Cost:$8-$10.
Total: ~636 calories.

14. Cuttlefish with pumpkin and potatoes
Ingredients
100 g cuttlefish already cleaned
50 g pumpkin already cleaned
½ tomato
35 g potatoes
1 clove garlic
 fresh parsley
 pepper to grind
 salt
 extra virgin olive oil
 turmeric powder
cuttlefish with pumpkin and potatoes
Preparation
Wash and peel the potatoes and steam them after cutting them into chunks. When they are ready, set them aside and continue with the other ingredients.
Wash the cuttlefish, cut them into regular pieces (not too small), set them aside, and refrigerate.

Wash the squash and cut it into pieces. Cook it in a large saucepan with the garlic clove, turmeric, tomato, a drizzle of extra virgin olive oil, and a little water.

Cook the squash for 10 minutes; add the cuttlefish and continue cooking over medium heat. Add the potatoes and mix everything when the cooking is almost finished. Season with salt and add pepper and a few clumps of fresh parsley.

Time:
25 minutes.
Estimated cost :
$8-$11
Total
730 calories

15. Grilled Salmon & Broccoli
Ingredients:
200g salmon (416 calories), 300g broccoli (102 calories), juice of 1 lemon (12 calories), 1g of salt (0 calories).
Preparation:
Grill the salmon and steam the broccoli. Drizzle with lemon juice and salt.

Time:
15 minutes.
Estimated Cost:
 $8-$10.
Total: ~530 calories. Pair it with a side of whole grains to meet the caloric requirement.

16. Turkey & Veggie Stir-fry

Ingredients:
200g turkey breast (296 calories), 300g mixed vegetables (150 calories), juice of 1 lemon (12 calories), and 1g of salt (0 calories).

Preparation:
Stir-fry the turkey and vegetables in a pan. Season with lemon juice and salt.

Time:
15 minutes.

Estimated Cost:
$6-$8.

Total: ~458 calories. Pair with a small portion of cooked quinoa to meet the caloric requirement.

17. Grilled Salmon & Green Beans

Ingredients:
200g salmon (416 calories), 300g green beans (93 calories), juice of 1 lemon (12 calories), 1g of salt (0 calories).

Preparation:
Grill the salmon and steam the green beans. Season with lemon juice and salt.

Time:
15 minutes.

Estimated Cost:
$8-$10.

Total: ~521 calories.
Add a serving of mixed nuts for protein and healthy fats to meet the caloric requirement.

18. Sardine and Kale Salad

Ingredients:

200g canned sardines in water (300 calories), 300g kale (150 calories), juice of 1 lemon (12 calories), and 1g of salt (0 calories).
Preparation:
Combine sardines, chopped kale in a bowl. Toss with lemon juice and salt.
Time:
10 minutes.
Estimated Cost:
$6-$8.
Total: ~462 calories.
Add a serving of mixed nuts (1/4 cup, ~200 calories) for healthy fats to meet the caloric requirement.

19. Tuna and Avocado Salad
Ingredients:
200g tuna steak (224 calories), 1 large avocado (320 calories), 200g mixed greens (40 calories), juice of 1 lemon (12 calories), and 1g of salt (0 calories).
Preparation:
 Grill the tuna steak and slice the avocado. Toss with mixed greens, lemon juice, and salt.
Time:
Time:
15 minutes.
Estimated Cost:
$10-$12.
Total: ~596 calories.

Add a small portion of rice (about 1.5 cups, ~324 calories) to meet the caloric requirement.

20. Sardines and Quinoa Salad

Ingredients:

200g canned sardines in water (300 calories), 300g mixed vegetables (150 calories), 1.5 cups cooked quinoa (333 calories), juice of 1 lemon (12 calories), and 1g of salt (0 calories).

Preparation:

Combine sardines, mixed vegetables, and quinoa in a bowl. Toss with lemon juice and salt.

Time:
10 minutes.
Estimated Cost:
$7-$9.
Total: ~795 calories.

21. Lean Beef with Sweet Potato

Ingredients:

200g lean beef (248 calories), 200g sweet potato (180 calories), 200g spinach (50 calories), juice of 1 lemon (12 calories), and 1g of salt (0 calories).

Preparation:

Grill the beef and bake the sweet potato. Serve with steamed spinach. Season with lemon juice and salt.

Time:
25 minutes.
Estimated Cost:
$10-$12.
Total: ~490 calories

. Serve with a large portion of cooked quinoa (~1.5 cups, ~333 calories) to meet the caloric requirement.

22. Chicken Breast with Broccoli
Ingredients:
200g chicken breast (330 calories), 300g broccoli (105 calories), juice of 1 lemon (12 calories), and 1g of salt (0 calories).
Preparation:
Grill the chicken breast and steam the broccoli. Season with lemon juice and salt.
Time:
20 minutes.
Estimated Cost:
$8-$10.
Total: 447 calories

23. Tuna and Quinoa Salad
Ingredients:
200g tuna steak (224 calories), 300g mixed vegetables (150 calories), 1.5 cups cooked quinoa (333 calories), juice of 1 lemon (12 calories), and 1g of salt (0 calories).
Preparation:
Grill the tuna steak. Toss with mixed vegetables, quinoa, lemon juice, and salt.
Time:
15 minutes.
Estimated Cost:
$10-$12.
Total: ~719 calories
Add a serving of mixed nuts (1/4 cup, ~200 calories) for healthy fats to meet the caloric requirement.

24. Baked Cod and Quinoa
Ingredients:
 200g cod (206 calories), 1.5 cups cooked quinoa (333 calories), 200g broccoli (70 calories), juice of 1 lemon (12 calories), and 1g of salt (0 calories).
Preparation:
Bake the cod, steam the broccoli. Serve with cooked quinoa. Season with lemon juice and salt.

Time:
20 minutes.
Estimated Cost:
$9-$11.
Total: ~621 calories.
 Add a small portion of cooked brown rice (about 1 cup, ~216 calories) to meet the caloric requirements.

25. Grilled Chicken with Tomato and Basil Salad
Ingredients:
200g grilled chicken breast (330 calories)
300g ripe tomatoes (60 calories)
A bunch of fresh basil leaves (1 calorie)
Juice of 1 lemon (12 calories)
1g of salt (0 calories)
Preparation:
 Season the chicken breast with half of the lemon juice and salt. Grill it on both sides until well cooked.
While the chicken grills, chop the tomatoes into chunks and tear the basil leaves.
Combine tomatoes and basil in a bowl. Add the rest of the lemon juice and salt. Mix well.
Serve the grilled chicken with the tomato and basil salad.

Time:
15 minutes.
Estimated Cost:
$7-$9.
Total: ~403 calories.

Add brown rice (1.5 cups, ~324 calories) and a small avocado (160 calories) to meet the caloric requirement.

Chapter 4
Vibrant Refreshers. Healthy Mid-Afternoon Delights

Welcome to the next delicious chapter of your culinary journey. This chapter is brimming with vibrant fruits, rich nuts, and occasional savory surprises that will turn your mid-afternoon snacking into a moment of joyful nourishment.

Snacks are pivotal in our day, providing the extra energy to carry us through until dinner. But in the name of health and especially for our friends combating cardiovascular diseases, we want to ensure these snacks are not just tasty but also nutritionally beneficial. They must balance carbohydrates, protein, and healthy fats to maintain strength and control hunger.

Our carefully curated snack recipes include portions of fruit for their natural sweetness and fiber, which slows the digestion of sugars, thereby preventing spikes in blood sugar levels. Moreover, fruits contain antioxidants and essential vitamins that support overall health, especially heart health.

Nuts are included for their protein and healthy fats, which provide satiety, curbing unnecessary cravings until dinner. Nuts like almonds, cashews, and walnuts are rich in unsaturated fats that can reduce harmful cholesterol levels and increase good cholesterol levels. They also contain Omega-3 fatty acids, a heart-healthy nutrient known for its inflammation-fighting powers. Now and then, we've also added a touch of Italian Grana Padano cheese, a protein and calcium product with unique flavors to elevate the pleasure of your mid-afternoon respite. This cheese is less fat than many others, making it a smart choice for cardiovascular health.

In this chapter, we've strived to achieve a celebration of wholesome, heart-friendly food that enlivens your palate and nourishes your body. These are recipes and steps towards a healthier lifestyle and a happier heart. They prove that eating for heart health does not require sacrifice; it opens up a world of vibrant, delicious possibilities. Enjoy these mid-afternoon delights, each offering approximately 200 calories, and transform your snacking habits into a feast of nutrition and flavor. Happy snacking!

Recipes

1. Apple & Almonds
- 1 medium apple (95 calories)
- 14g almonds (80 calories)

2. Pear & Walnuts
- 1 medium pear (102 calories)
- 14g walnuts (90 calories)

3. Grapes & Cashews
- 1 cup of grapes (104 calories)
- 10g cashews (60 calories)

4. Nectarine & Pistachios
- 1 large nectarine (70 calories)
- 20g pistachios (115 calories)

5. Peach & Hazelnuts
- 1 giant peach (70 calories)
- 18g hazelnuts (115 calories)

6. Berries & Pecans
- 1 cup of mixed berries (70 calories)
- 14g pecans (100 calories)

7. Melon & Macadamias
- 1 cup of melon cubes (60 calories)
- 10g macadamias (75 calories)
- 20g Grana Padano cheese (60 calories)

8. Pineapple & Brazil Nuts
- 1 cup of pineapple chunks (80 calories)

- 16g Brazil nuts (105 calories)

9. Kiwi & Peanuts
- 2 medium kiwi (90 calories)
- 14g peanuts (90 calories)

10. Banana & Almonds
- 1 medium banana (105 calories)
- 10g almonds (60 calories)
- 20g Grana Padano cheese (70 calories)

11. Orange & Pistachios
- 1 medium orange (62 calories)
- 20g pistachios (115 calories)

12. Strawberry & Walnuts
- 1 cup of strawberries (53 calories)
- 20g walnuts (131 calories)

13. Raspberry & Cashews
- 1 cup of raspberries (64 calories)
- 20g cashews (117 calories)

14. Blueberry & Hazelnuts
- 1 cup of blueberries (85 calories)
- 15g hazelnuts (100 calories)

15. Mango & Macadamias
- 1 cup of mango (99 calories)
- 10g macadamias (75 calories)
- 20g Grana Padano cheese (70 calories)

16. Cherry & Brazil Nuts
- 1 cup of cherries (97 calories)

- 12g Brazil nuts (88 calories)

17. Plum & Peanuts
- 2 medium plums (76 calories)
- 15g peanuts (90 calories)

18. Apricot & Almonds
- 3 medium apricots (51 calories)
- 20g almonds (115 calories)

19. Blackberry & Pistachios
- 1 cup of blackberries (62 calories)
- 20g pistachios (115 calories)

20. Guava & Walnuts
- 1 medium guava (38 calories)
- 25g walnuts (160 calories)

21. Papaya & Cashews
- 1 cup of papaya (62 calories)
- 20g cashews (117 calories)

22. Avocado & Hazelnuts
- Half a medium avocado (120 calories)
- 12g hazelnuts (75 calories)

23. Cantaloupe & Macadamias
- 1 cup of cantaloupe (60 calories)
- 15g macadamias (115 calories)

24. Pomegranate & Brazil Nuts
- Half a pomegranate (83 calories)
- 16g Brazil nuts (105 calories)

25. Watermelon & Peanuts
- 1 cup of watermelon (46 calories)
- 20g peanuts (113 calories)
- 10g Grana Padano cheese (40 calories)

Chapter 5
Evening. A symphony of delicacies for a healthy dinner.

As dusk unveils the starry night sky, another kind of magic stirs in our kitchens. It's time for dinner! A harmonious blend of nourishment and comfort, dinner is a beacon of warmth at the end of a long day. This chapter reveals a captivating array of dishes designed to make your evenings shine with health, taste, and joy.

We understand that every meal is crucial to your health and well-being. For this reason, our recipes meticulously ensure a balanced calorie intake. We guarantee the satiety of a hearty meal carefully aligned with your nutritional needs.

Repetition can fade the liveliest of culinary adventures. That's why we bring a treasure trove of variety to the table, from the juiciness of white meats and the richness of the ocean to the earthy goodness of an array of vegetables.

Our dishes are made with the utmost simplicity, following a preparation time of 15-30 minutes, except for one perhaps that needs more time. In addition, we have stated the estimated cost of each recipe to help you maintain a balanced budget without compromising health or taste.

We have replaced traditional oil-based seasonings with the tangy appeal of lemon juice whenever possible, enhancing your dishes' flavor profile and nutritional value. This simple but powerful practical amplifies the intrinsic taste of ingredients while providing essential vitamins.

This chapter is a heartfelt ode to heart health that unfolds through delicious dinner recipes. It is a culinary canvas to explore and paint with your unique strokes.

So let us embark on this fascinating gastronomic journey.

1. Grilled Salmon & Quinoa

Ingredients:

200g Salmon fillet (360 calories)

1 cup Quinoa (220 calories)

Steamed broccoli (55 calories)

Lemon wedge (3 calories)

Salt (0 calories)

Pepper (0 calories)

Preparation:

Season the salmon fillet, grill it for 10-12 minutes. Cook Quinoa according to package instructions. Serve salmon over Quinoa with steamed broccoli on the side. Squeeze the lemon wedge over the salmon.

Time:

20 minutes

Estimated Cost:

$12

Total Calories: 638

2. Shrimp & Vegetable Pasta

Ingredients:

200g Shrimp (226 calories)

2 cups of cooked whole wheat pasta (348 calories)

Mixed vegetables (bell peppers, cherry tomatoes) (75 calories)

1 tbsp Olive oil (119 calories)
Salt (0 calories)
Pepper (0 calories)

Preparation:
Place olive oil in a frying pan and cook over low heat for a few minutes.
Add the vegetables and cook for a few minutes.
Season with salt and pepper.
Serve the shrimp and vegetables over the pasta cooked in the other skillet.
Italian durum wheat penne pasta is recommended.

Time:
20 minutes
Estimated Cost:
 $10
Total Calories: 768

3. Seared Tuna with Couscous

Ingredients:
200g Tuna Steak (240 calories)
1 cup Cooked Couscous (176 calories)
Mixed Salad Greens (10 calories)
Lemon Juice (10 calories)
Salt (0 calories)
Pepper (0 calories)

Preparation:

Blanch the tuna steak on each side for 2-3 minutes (depending on thickness) in a skillet, again over low heat. Meanwhile, you have cooked the couscous semolina. Serve it with cooked Couscous, mixed salad, and a squeeze of lemon.

Time:
20 minutes
Estimated Cost:
$14
Total Calories: 436

4. Beef Stew with Sweet Potatoes

Ingredients:
200g Lean Beef cut into cubes (250 calories)
1 Medium Sweet Potato, cubed (103 calories)
Mixed Vegetables (carrots, peas, onions) (150 calories)
1 tbsp Olive Oil (119 calories)
Salt (0 calories)
Pepper (0 calories)

Preparation:
After heating some olive oil in a pot, add the beef and cook until golden brown. Add vegetables first, cut into chunks and sweet potato, cover with enough water, boil, and simmer until vegetables are tender.

Time:
25 minutes
Estimated Cost:
$12
Total Calories: 622

5. Lemon and herb chicken with spinach salad

Ingredients:
200 g chicken breast (330 calories)
2 cups of spinach (14 calories)
Lemon juice (10 calories)
1 tablespoon olive oil (119 calories)
Salt (0 calories)
Pepper (0 calories)

Preparation:
Season chicken with lemon juice, salt, and pepper. Grill the meat until cooked through. Boil spinach until cooked through and drain. Serve with a spinach salad dressed with olive oil, salt and pepper.

Time:
15 minutes
Estimated cost:
$10
Total calories: 473

6. Spicy cod with Quinoa
Ingredients:
200 g cod fillet (186 calories)
1 cup of cooked Quinoa (222 calories)
Mixed vegetable salad (10 calories)
Lemon juice (10 calories)
1 tablespoon olive oil (119 calories)
Chili flakes (5 calories)
Salt (0 calories)

Preparation:
Season cod with lemon juice, chili flakes, and salt. Grill cod until cooked through. Serve with pre-cooked Quinoa and a vegetable salad dressed with olive oil.

Time:
20 minutes
Estimated cost:
$10
Total calories: 552

7. Baked salmon with mashed sweet potatoes
Ingredients:
200 g salmon fillet (367 calories)
1 medium sweet potato (103 calories)
1 teaspoon olive oil (40 calories)
Steamed green beans (44 calories)

Salt (0 calories)
Pepper (0 calories)

Preparation:
Bake the salmon at 180°C (350°F) until the desired doneness. Meanwhile, steam the sweet potato, and mash it with olive oil, salt, and pepper. Serve the salmon with the mashed sweet potato and previously cooked green beans.

Time:
30 minutes
Estimated cost:
$14
Total calories: 554

8. Stir-fried turkey with brown rice
Ingredients:
200 g sliced turkey breast (268 calories)
1 cup cooked brown rice (216 calories)
Stir-fried mixed vegetables (150 calories)
1 tablespoon soy sauce (9 calories)
1 tablespoon olive oil (40 calories)
Salt (0 calories)
Pepper (0 calories)

Preparation:
Put oil in a skillet over low heat, add turkey, and cook until golden brown. Add sautéed vegetables to another skillet, and sauté until tender. Serve with cooked brown rice and a drizzle of soy sauce.

Time:
20 minutes
Estimated cost:
$11
Total calories:
683

9. Grilled Tuna Steak with Bulgur Wheat Salad

Ingredients:
200 g tuna steak (288 calories)
1 cup cooked bulgur (151 calories)
Mixed vegetable salad (10 calories)
Lemon juice (10 calories)
2 tablespoons olive oil (238 calories)
Salt (0 calories)
Pepper (0 calories)

Preparation:
Season tuna with salt, pepper, and lemon juice, then grill. Mix the bulgur with the salad greens, lemon juice, and olive oil. Serve with the grilled tuna on top.

Time:
20 minutes
Estimated cost:
$14
Total calories:
697

10. Risotto with chicken and mushrooms
Ingredients:
200 g skinless chicken breast (330 calories)
1 cup cooked risotto rice (169 calories)
1 cup sliced mushrooms (15 calories)
1 tablespoon olive oil (119 calories)
1/2 cup low-sodium chicken broth (7.5 calories)
Salt (0 calories)
Pepper (0 calories)

Preparation:
In a skillet, sauté chicken and mushrooms in olive oil until cooked. Add the risotto rice and gradually pour in chicken broth, stirring constantly, until the rice is creamy and cooked. Season with salt and pepper.

Time:
25 minutes
Estimated cost:
$12

Total calories: 640

11. Baked cod with ratatouille
Ingredients:
200 g cod fillet (186 calories)
1 cup ratatouille (175 calories)
Lemon juice (10 calories)
1 tablespoon olive oil (119 calories)
Salt (0 calories)
Pepper (0 calories)

Preparation:
Season the cod with salt, pepper, and lemon juice, then bake in a 180-degree oven until golden brown. Heat the ratatouille in a skillet with a bit of olive oil. Serve the baked cod with the ratatouille on the side.

Time:
30 minutes
Estimated cost:
$12
Total calories: 490

12. Seared salmon with quinoa salad
Ingredients:
200 g salmon fillet (367 calories)

1 cup of cooked Quinoa (220 calories)
Mixed vegetable salad (10 calories)
Lemon juice (10 calories)
2 tablespoons olive oil (238 calories)
Salt (0 calories)
Pepper (0 calories)

Preparation:
Season salmon with salt and pepper, and blanch in one tablespoon of olive oil in a skillet until cooked. Mix Quinoa with salad greens, lemon juice, and 1 tablespoon olive oil. Serve with seared salmon on top.

Time:
20 minutes
Estimated cost:
$15
Total calories: 845

13. Stir-fried turkey with brown rice
Ingredients:
200 g turkey breast (286 calories)
1 cup cooked brown rice (215 calories)
Stir-fried mixed vegetables (100 calories)
2 tablespoons soy sauce (18 calories)
1 tablespoon olive oil (119 calories)
Salt (0 calories)

Pepper (0 calories)

Preparation:

Sauté turkey and vegetables in olive oil until cooked through. Add soy sauce, salt, and pepper. Serve sautéed vegetables and turkey over cooked brown rice.

Time:
15 minutes
Estimated cost:
$12
Total calories: 738

14. Grilled mackerel with roasted vegetables

Ingredients:
200 g mackerel fillet (458 calories)
Roasted mixed vegetables (150 calories)
Lemon juice (10 calories)
1 tablespoon olive oil (119 calories)
Salt (0 calories)
Pepper (0 calories

Preparation:
Season the mackerel with salt, pepper, and lemon juice, then grill over charcoal or in an oven. Toss vegetables in olive oil and roast until tender. Serve the grilled mackerel with the roasted vegetables on the side.

Time:
30 minutes
Estimated cost:
$12
Total calories: 737

15. Mustard chicken with steamed vegetables

Ingredients:
200 g chicken breast (330 calories)
Steamed mixed vegetables (150 calories)
1 tablespoon honey (64 calories)
1 tablespoon of mustard (10 calories)
Salt (0 calories)
Pepper (0 calories)

Preparation:
Season chicken with salt, pepper, honey, and mustard, then bake until cooked. Serve with steamed vegetables on the side.

Time:
20 minutes
Estimated cost:

$10
Total calories: 554

16. Baked cod with sweet potato fries
Ingredients:
200 g cod fillet (206 calories)
200 g sweet potatoes (180 calories)
1 tablespoon olive oil (119 calories)
Lemon juice (10 calories)
Salt (0 calories)
Pepper (0 calories)

Preparation:
Season cod with lemon juice, salt, and pepper, then bake. Toss sweet potato fries in seed oil and cook well until crispy. Serve the baked cod with sweet potato fries on the side.

Time:
30 minutes
Estimated cost:
$12
Total calories: 515

17. Turkey tacos

Ingredients:

200 g turkey breast (286 calories)

2 small corn tortillas (100 calories)

Lettuce (5 calories)

Tomato (11 calories)

Onion (20 calories)

1 tablespoon olive oil (119 calories)

Salt (0 calories)

Pepper (0 calories)

Preparation:

Sauté turkey with onion in olive oil in a skillet over low heat. Season to taste with salt and pepper. Prepare tacos on the side with sautéed turkey, lettuce, and sliced Tomato.

Time:

15 minutes

Estimated cost:

$10

Total calories: 541

18. Chicken and vegetable stir-fry

Ingredients:

200 g chicken breast (330 calories)

Mixed vegetables (carrots, peppers, zucchini) (80 calories)

1 tablespoon soy sauce (9 calories)

1 tablespoon olive oil (119 calories)
Salt (0 calories)
Pepper (0 calories)

Preparation:
Place olive oil in a wok or large skillet and heat it. Add the shredded chicken and cook until cooked through. Add the previously boiled vegetables and stir-fry until tender. Drizzle with soy sauce.

Time:
15 minutes
Estimated cost:
$10
Total calories: 538

19. Steamed Cod with Bell Peppers
Ingredients:
200g Cod (186 calories)
200g Bell Peppers (92 calories)
1 Lemon (12 calories)
Salt (0 calories)
Pepper (0 calories)

Preparation:

Season the cod with salt, pepper, and lemon juice. Steam the cod until it's cooked through. Meanwhile, slice the bell peppers and sauté them until they're tender. Serve the steamed cod with the sautéed bell peppers.

Time:
15 minutes
Estimated Cost:
$12
Total Calories: 290

20. Grilled Chicken with Asparagus
Ingredients:
200g Chicken Breast (330 calories)
200g Asparagus (80 calories)
1 Lemon (12 calories)
Salt (0 calories)
Pepper (0 calories)
Preparation:
Season the salmon with salt and pepper and grill until cooked through.
Grill asparagus until tender.
Place grilled chicken on the table with asparagus and a squeeze of lemon juice.

Time:

20 minutes
Estimated Cost:
$10 Total
Total Calories: 422

21. Baked Salmon with Brussels Sprouts

Ingredients:

200g Salmon (367 calories)

200g Brussels Sprouts (86 calories)

1 Lemon (12 calories)

Salt (0 calories)

Pepper (0 calories)

Preparation:

Season the salmon with salt and pepper. Add a squeeze of lemon juice. Bake the salmon at 200 degrees for 12 to 15 minutes or until the fish is cooked. Meanwhile, steam the Brussels sprouts. Serve the baked salmon with the sprouts.

Time:

20 minutes

Estimated Cost:

$14

Total Calories: 465

22. Poached Salmon and Steamed Broccoli
Ingredients:
200g Salmon (414 calories)
300g Broccoli (105 calories)
1 Lemon (12 calories)
Salt (0 calories)
Pepper (0 calories)

Preparation:
Put salt and pepper on the salmon and begin poaching until done. Poaching salmon means cooking it inside a pot with water on low heat for at least 45 minutes. Meanwhile, steam the broccoli until tender. Finally, serve the salmon with broccoli and a squeeze of lemon juice.

Time: 45 minutes
Estimated Cost: $12
Total Calories: 531

23. Grilled Sardines and Quinoa Salad
Ingredients:
200g Sardines (292 calories)
100g Quinoa, cooked (120 calories)
100g Mixed Salad Greens (14 calories)

Salt to taste (0 calories)
Pepper to taste (0 calories)
1 Lemon (12 calories)

Preparation:
Grill the sardines until fully cooked. Mix the cooked quinoa with the salad greens, which have been prepared in the meantime. Then put in salt, pepper, and lemon juice. Serve the sardines on top of the quinoa salad.

Time: 15 minutes
Estimated Cost: $10
Total Calories: 438

24. Grilled chicken with ratatouille
Ingredients:
200 g chicken breast (220 kcal)
1 teaspoon olive oil (40 kcal)
1/2 teaspoon salt (0 kcal)
1 medium zucchini (31 kcal)
1 red bell pepper (37 kcal)
1 small eggplant (35 kcal)
2 tomatoes (44 kcal)
1 small onion (28 kcal)
2 cloves of garlic (9 kcal)
2 tablespoons chopped fresh basil (1 kcal)
1 teaspoon chopped fresh thyme (1 kcal)
1 tablespoon lemon juice (4 kcal)

Preparation:
Heat grill or skillet. Add 1/2 teaspoon salt or oil to chicken. Grill until the meat is well done. While the chicken is grilling, cut all vegetables into similar-sized pieces. In a large skillet, sauté the onion and garlic until softened. Add the eggplant, zucchini, and peppers. Cook until vegetables begin to soften. Add the tomatoes, fresh herbs, remaining salt, and lemon juice. Let cook until the vegetables are chunky.
Serve the grilled chicken with the ratatouille on the side.

Time 35 minutes
Estimated cost: $7
Total calories: 450 kcal

25. Baked salmon with sweet potatoes and asparagus
Ingredients:
200 g salmon fillet (367 kcal)
1 medium sweet potato (103 kcal)
10 Asparagus (32 kcal)
1 tablespoon olive oil (120 kcal)
1/2 tablespoon salt (0 kcal)
1 tablespoon lemon juice (4 kcal)

Preparation:

Turn the oven to 200°C (392°F). Place aluminum foil or baking paper in the bottom of a baking dish. Cut the potato into small pieces and brown it with a little olive oil and a pinch of salt.

Arrange the salmon fillet and asparagus in the oven. Drizzle with the remaining olive oil and sprinkle with a little salt. Bake for about 20 minutes, or until the salmon is cooked through and the potato is tender.

Time: 30 minutes
Estimated cost: $9
Total calories: 626 kcal

Chapter 6
One hundred snack ideas to stop hunger with healthy food.

Whole Grain Toast with Almond Butter - One slice of whole grain toast (70 calories) spread with 1 tbsp almond butter (98 calories) and sprinkled with a pinch of chia seeds (20 calories). Total: 188 calories.

Greek Yogurt with Honey and Walnuts - 1/2 cup of non-fat Greek yogurt (65 calories), drizzled with 1 tsp of honey (20 calories), and topped with 1 tbsp chopped walnuts (45 calories). Total: 130 calories.

Apple and Cheese - One medium apple (95 calories) with 1 oz of low-fat cheddar cheese (50 calories). Total: 145 calories.

Cucumber and Hummus - One medium cucumber (45 calories) sliced and served with 2 tbsp of hummus (70 calories). Total: 115 calories.

Hard-Boiled Egg with Whole Grain Crackers - One hard-boiled egg (70 calories) with five whole-grain crackers (100 calories). Total: 170 calories.

Mixed Berries and Almonds - 1/2 cup of mixed berries (40 calories) and 10 raw almonds (70 calories). Total: 110 calories.

Avocado on Rice Cake - Half an avocado (120 calories) spread on one brown rice cake (35 calories). Total: 155 calories.

Peanut Butter and Banana - One small banana (90 calories) with 1 tbsp of peanut butter (90 calories). Total: 180 calories.

Cherry Tomatoes with Mozzarella - One cup of cherry tomatoes (30 calories) with 1 oz of mozzarella cheese (70 calories). Total: 100 calories.

Vegetable Sticks with Cottage Cheese - One cup of raw vegetable sticks (carrots, bell peppers) (50 calories) served with 1/2 cup of low-fat cottage cheese (80 calories). Total: 130 calories.

Celery and Peanut Butter - Two medium celery sticks (15 calories) spread with 1 tbsp peanut butter (90 calories). Total: 105 calories.

Rye Crispbread with Avocado - One rye crispbread (35 calories) topped with 1/4 of an avocado (60 calories). Total: 95 calories.

Carrot Sticks with Hummus - One medium carrot (25 calories) cut into sticks and served with 1 tbsp of hummus (35 calories). Total: 60 calories.

Melon and Prosciutto - One cup of melon cubes (60 calories) wrapped in 1 oz of prosciutto (50 calories). Total: 110 calories.

Greek Yogurt with Berries - One small container (150g) of non-fat Greek yogurt (80 calories) topped with 1 cup of mixed berries (80 calories). Total: 160 calories.

Almonds and Dried Apricots - 10 raw almonds (70 calories) and three dried apricot halves (60 calories). Total: 130 calories.

Apple Slices with Almond Butter - One small apple (55 calories) sliced and served with 1 tbsp of almond butter (98 calories). Total: 153 calories.

Cottage Cheese with Pineapple - One small container (150g) of low-fat cottage cheese (80 calories) topped with 1/2 cup of chopped pineapple (40 calories). Total: 120 calories.

Bell Pepper with Guacamole - One medium bell pepper (25 calories) cut into strips and served with 1/4 cup of guacamole (60 calories). Total: 85 calories.

Tuna Salad Celery Sticks - Two medium celery sticks (15 calories) filled with a mixture of 2 oz of canned tuna (60 calories) and 1 tbsp of light mayonnaise (40 calories). Total: 115 calories.

Cucumber and Cottage Cheese - Half a large cucumber (23 calories) sliced and topped with 1/2 cup of low-fat cottage cheese (80 calories). Total: 103 calories.

Boiled Egg with Cherry Tomatoes - One hard-boiled egg (68 calories) served with a cup of cherry tomatoes (30 calories). Total: 98 calories.

Peach and Ricotta Toast - One slice of whole grain toast (70 calories) topped with 1/4 cup of part-skim ricotta cheese (85 calories) and half a medium peach (30 calories). Total: 185 calories.

Greek Yogurt and Cucumber Dip - Half a cup of non-fat Greek yogurt (65 calories) mixed with a quarter of a large cucumber (11 calories), served as a dip with a medium carrot (25 calories). Total: 101 calories.

Tuna and Cucumber Slices - Half a cup of tuna (90 calories) served with half a large cucumber (23 calories). Total: 113 calories.

Apple and Peanut Butter - Half a large apple (60 calories) served with a tablespoon of peanut butter (90 calories). Total: 150 calories.

Cherry Tomatoes and Mozzarella Sticks - A cup of cherry tomatoes (30 calories) served with two part-skim mozzarella sticks (100 calories). Total: 130 calories.

Oatmeal and Berries - Half a cup of cooked oatmeal (80 calories) topped with half a cup of mixed berries (40 calories). Total: 120 calories.

Pear and Almond Butter - Half a large pear (57 calories) served with a tablespoon of almond butter (98 calories). Total: 155 calories.

Hummus and Bell Pepper Sticks - Half a cup of bell pepper sticks (15 calories) served with two tablespoons of hummus (70 calories). Total: 85 calories.

Balsamic Strawberries and Ricotta - 1 cup of strawberries (53 calories) topped with 2 tablespoons of part-skim ricotta (39 calories) and a drizzle of balsamic glaze (30 calories). Total: 122 calories.

Grana Padano and Apple Slices - 1 oz Grana Padano cheese (120 calories) with half a large apple (60 calories). Total: 180 calories.

Mozzarella and Tomato Skewers - 1 oz part-skim mozzarella (70 calories) and one medium Tomato (22 calories), cut into pieces and skewered. Drizzle with a teaspoon of balsamic vinegar (5 calories). Total: 97 calories.

Pear and Pecorino - Half a pear (51 calories) served with 1 oz of Pecorino Romano cheese (110 calories). Total: 161 calories.

Ricotta and Honey Toast - One slice of whole-grain bread (70 calories) topped with 1 tablespoon of part-skim ricotta (39 calories) and a drizzle of honey (20 calories). Total: 129 calories.

Parmesan Popcorn - 2 cups of air-popped popcorn (62 calories) sprinkled with 2 tablespoons of grated cheese (42 calories). Total: 104 calories.

Bell Peppers and Feta - 1 cup of sliced bell peppers (30 calories) served with 1 oz of feta cheese (75 calories). Total: 105 calories.

Gorgonzola and Walnut Stuffed Dates - Two Medjool dates (132 calories) stuffed with 1 teaspoon of gorgonzola cheese (40 calories) and 2 walnut halves (26 calories). Total: 198 calories.

Caprese Bites - One medium Tomato (22 calories), 1 oz of part-skim mozzarella (70 calories), and 1/4 cup of fresh basil (1 calorie) skewered and drizzled with 1 teaspoon of balsamic vinegar (5 calories). Total: 98 calories.

Zucchini and Parmesan Bites - 1 medium zucchini (31 calories) cut into slices, topped with 2 tablespoons of grated Parmesan cheese (42 calories), and broiled until the cheese is bubbly. Total: 73

Carrot and Hummus Roll-Ups - One medium carrot (25 calories) thinly sliced and spread with 2 tablespoons of hummus (70 calories). Roll up and enjoy. Total: 95 calories.

Grana Padano & Apricots - 1 oz Grana Padano cheese (120 calories) paired with two fresh apricots (34 calories). Total: 154 calories.

Almond & Orange Snack - 10 raw almonds (70 calories) with a tiny orange (60 calories). Total: 130 calories.

Greek Yogurt & Honey - Half a cup of non-fat Greek yogurt (65 calories) with a teaspoon of honey (20 calories). Total: 85 calories.

Parmesan Kale Chips - 2 cups of kale (66 calories) tossed with a teaspoon of olive oil (40 calories) and a tablespoon of Parmesan cheese (22 calories), then baked. Total: 128 calories.

Mozzarella & Cherry Tomato Skewers - 1 oz part-skim mozzarella cheese (70 calories) and five cherry tomatoes (15 calories) on a skewer. Total: 85 calories.

Blue Cheese Stuffed Apricots - Three dried apricots (51 calories) stuffed with 1 oz of blue cheese (100 calories). Total: 151 calories.

Balsamic Fig & Ricotta Toast - One slice of whole-grain bread (70 calories) topped with 1 tablespoon of part-skim ricotta cheese (39 calories) and one fresh fig (30 calories) sliced and drizzled with balsamic glaze (30 calories). Total: 169 calories.

Pecorino & Almond Stuffed Dates - Two Medjool dates (132 calories) stuffed with 1 oz of Pecorino Romano cheese (110 calories) and two almonds (14 calories). Total: 256 calories.

Parmesan & Rosemary Popcorn - 2 cups of air-popped popcorn (62 calories) sprinkled with a tablespoon of Parmesan cheese (22 calories) and a sprinkle of dried rosemary. Total: 84 calories.

Tuna and Crackers - A small can of light tuna (100 calories) mixed with a teaspoon of creamy mayo (15 calories) served with 6 whole-grain crackers (70 calories). Total: 185 calories.

Peanut Butter Celery Sticks - Two celery sticks (20 calories) filled with a tablespoon of peanut butter (90 calories). Total: 110 calories.

Cottage Cheese and Cantaloupe - Half a cup of low-fat cottage cheese (80 calories) served with half a cup of cubes (30 calories). Total: 110 calories.

Grana Padano & Pear Slices - 1 oz Grana Padano cheese (120 calories) paired with half a pear (50 calories). Total: 170 calories.

Avocado Rice Cakes - One rice cake (70 calories) topped with a quarter of an avocado (60 calories), sprinkled with sea salt and chili flakes. Total: 130 calories.

Apple & Almond Butter - One small apple (80 calories) sliced and served with a tablespoon of almond butter (100 calories). Total: 180 calories.

Protein Smoothie - Blend a scoop of protein powder (100 calories) with a cup of unsweetened almond milk (30 calories). Total: 130 calories.

Italian Cheese & Olives - 1 oz Italian cheese (110 calories) served with 10 olives (50 calories). Total: 160 calories.

Greek Yogurt & Berries - Half a cup of non-fat Greek yogurt (65 calories) topped with a quarter cup of mixed berries (20 calories). Total: 85 calories.

Banana & Peanut Butter - One small banana (90 calories) served with a tablespoon of peanut butter (90 calories). Total: 180 calories.

Ricotta & Honey Toast - One slice of whole grain bread (70 calories) topped with a tablespoon of part-skim ricotta cheese (39 calories) and drizzled with a teaspoon of honey (20 calories). Total: 129 calories.

Mozzarella & Tomato - 1 oz part-skim mozzarella cheese (70 calories) served with one medium Tomato (22 calories), sprinkled with basil and a pinch of salt. Total: 92 calories.

Boiled Egg & Spinach - One boiled egg (78 calories) served with a cup of raw spinach (7 calories), dressed with a teaspoon of balsamic vinegar (5 calories). Total: 90 calories.

Strawberries & Cream Cheese - Six strawberries (36 calories) served with two tablespoons of light cream cheese (70 calories). Total: 106 calories.

Almonds & Dried Cranberries - 10 raw almonds (70 calories) paired with a tablespoon of dried cranberries (45 calories). Total: 115 calories.

Cherry Tomatoes & Hummus - 10 cherry tomatoes (30 calories) served with two tablespoons (70 calories). Total: 100 calories.

Kiwi & Greek Yogurt - One medium kiwi (42 calories) served with a half cup of non-fat Greek yogurt (65 calories). Total: 107 calories.

Rye Crackers & Avocado - Two rye crackers (70 calories) topped with a quarter of an avocado (60 calories). Total: 130 calories.

Grana Padano & Apple - 1 oz Grana Padano cheese (120 calories) paired with half an apple (40 calories). Total: 160 calories.

Edamame - Half a cup of cooked edamame (100 calories) sprinkled with a pinch of salt. Total: 100 calories.

Carrots & Tzatziki - One medium carrot (25 calories) served with two tablespoons of tzatziki sauce (60 calories). Total: 85 calories.

Cucumber & Cottage Cheese - Half a cucumber (23 calories) served with a quarter cup of low-fat cottage cheese (40 calories). Total: 63 calories.

Bell Pepper & Guacamole - One medium bell pepper (24 calories) served with two tablespoons of guacamole (100 calories). Total: 124 calories.

Peach & Ricotta - One medium peach (60 calories) served with two tablespoons of part-skim ricotta cheese (78 calories). Total: 138 calories.

Baked Kale Chips - One cup of kale (34 calories) tossed in a teaspoon of olive oil (40 calories) and baked until crispy. Total: 74 calories.

Italian Cheese & Grapes - 1 oz Italian cheese (110 calories) served with half a cup of grapes (52 calories). Total: 162 calories.

Popcorn - Three cups of air-popped popcorn (90 calories) lightly sprinkled with sea salt. Total: 90 calories.

Dates & Almonds - Two Medjool dates (133 calories) stuffed with two almonds (28 calories). Total: 161 calories.

Celery & Cream Cheese - Two celery sticks (20 calories) filled with two tablespoons of light cream cheese (70 calories). Total: 90 calories.

Apple & Cheddar - Half an apple (40 calories) served with 1 oz cheddar cheese (110 calories). Total: 150 calories.

Pear & Provolone - Half a pear (51 calories) paired with 1 oz Provolone cheese (98 calories). Total: 149 calories.

Watermelon & Feta - One cup of watermelon (46 calories) served with 1 oz of Feta cheese (75 calories). Total: 121 calories.

Radishes & Butter - Four radishes (8 calories) with one teaspoon of butter (34 calories). Total: 42 calories.

Cantaloupe & Greek Yogurt - One cup of cantaloupe (54 calories) served with a half cup of non-fat Greek yogurt (65 calories). Total: 119 calories.

Apricot & Almonds - Two apricots (34 calories) and six almonds (42 calories). Total: 76 calories.

Spinach & Feta Roll-up - One cup of spinach (7 calories) with 1 oz feta cheese (75 calories) in a small whole grain tortilla (70 calories). Total: 152 calories.

Strawberries & Cream - Half a cup of strawberries (24 calories) served with two tablespoons of whipped cream (51 calories). Total: 75 calories.

Grana Padano & Pear - 1 oz Grana Padano cheese (120 calories) paired with half a pear (51 calories). Total: 171 calories.

Cherry Tomatoes & Mozzarella - Half a cup of cherry tomatoes (25 calories) served with 1 oz of fresh mozzarella cheese (70 calories). Total: 95 calories.

Cucumber & Hummus - One medium cucumber (45 calories) served with two tablespoons of hummus (70 calories). Total: 115 calories.

Blueberries & Greek Yogurt - Half a cup of blueberries (42 calories) served with a half cup of non-fat Greek yogurt (65 calories). Total: 107 calories.

Italian Cheese & Apricots - 1 oz Italian cheese (110 calories) served with two apricots (34 calories). Total: 144 calories.

Asparagus & Hollandaise - Four asparagus spears (13 calories) served with one tablespoon of hollandaise sauce (67 calories). Total: 80 calories.

Ricotta & Honey - Two tablespoons of part-skim ricotta cheese (78 calories) served with one teaspoon of honey (21 calories). Total: 99 calories.

Olives & Feta - Five olives (25 calories) served with 1 oz of Feta cheese (75 calories). Total: 100 calories.

Kiwi & Almond Butter - One medium kiwi (42 calories) with one teaspoon of almond butter (34 calories). Total: 76 calories.

Zucchini & Hummus Dip - One medium zucchini (33 calories) cut into sticks and served with two tablespoons of hummus (70 calories). Total: 103 calories.

Cherry & Ricotta - Half a cup of cherries (52 calories) served with two tablespoons of part-skim ricotta cheese (39 calories). Total: 91 calories.

Apple Slices & Cheddar - Half a medium apple (52 calories) served with 1 oz of cheddar cheese (113 calories). Total: 165 calories.

Bell Pepper & Guacamole - Half a bell pepper (18 calories) served with two tablespoons of guacamole (50 calories). Total: 68 calories.

Chapter 7

12 Weeks of Nourishing Recipes. A Comprehensive Meal Plan for a Heart-Healthy Life

In this chapter, we embark together on a 90-day culinary journey, a full three months of delicious and balanced meals that promote a healthier lifestyle while making your taste buds rejoice. This section of the book serves as a roadmap, guiding you to a future where heart health is no longer a distant goal, but a leisurely journey filled with variety and flavor.

We have curated a myriad of recipes that span every corner of the culinary world, from hearty breakfasts to satiating evening snacks and everything in between. You'll explore a cornucopia of fresh fruits, nutrient-dense vegetables, lean proteins, and heart-healthy fats with our selection of more than a hundred recipes designed to keep you engaged, excited, and most importantly, nourished.

This eating plan is designed for those leading a predominantly sedentary lifestyle, with a daily caloric intake of about 1900-2000 kilocalories. These values are based on general guidelines, and personal needs may vary depending on individual metabolic rate, activity level, age, and gender. For those with higher energy needs, we recommend adding more fruit, snacks, or slightly larger portions to each meal while maintaining the same balanced macronutrient ratio.

One of the strengths of this chapter is its flexibility. Feel free to swap recipes from day to day, substitute ingredients, and change portions to suit your tastes and nutritional needs. Our goal is to provide you with the tools and knowledge you need to cultivate a healthier lifestyle, not to impose an inflexible dietary regimen on you.

So as you embark on this 90-day culinary expedition, remember to savor every bite, relish the variety and, most importantly, listen to your body. It's not about perfection, it's about progression. Here is heart-healthy living, one delicious meal at a time.

Recommended water intake: at least 2 liters a day.

Week 1

Monday
- **Breakfast:** Oatmeal with Berries and Almonds (250 kcal)
- Morning Snack: Greek Yogurt with Honey and Walnuts (200 kcal)
- Lunch: Mediterranean Tuna Salad (600 kcal)
- Afternoon Snack: Carrot Sticks with Hummus (150 kcal)
- Dinner: Grilled Chicken with Ratatouille (450 kcal)
- Evening Snack: Apple with Peanut Butter (100 kcal)

Tuesday
- Breakfast: Egg White Omelet with Veggies (300 kcal)
- Morning Snack: Banana with Almond Butter (200 kcal)
- Lunch: Cod and Veggie Stir Fry (600 kcal)
- Afternoon Snack: Grapes and Cheese (150 kcal)
- Dinner: Baked Salmon with Sweet Potato and Asparagus (626 kcal)
- Evening Snack: Handful of almonds (100 kcal)

Wednesday
- Breakfast: Greek Yogurt Parfait (250 kcal)
- Morning Snack: Handful of Almonds and a Banana (200 kcal)
- Lunch: Greek Chicken Salad (600 kcal)
- Afternoon Snack: Apple and Peanut Butter (150 kcal)
- Dinner: Grilled Tuna with Quinoa Salad (650 kcal)
- Evening Snack: Greek Yogurt with Honey (100 kcal)

Thursday
- Breakfast: Oatmeal with Berries and Almonds (250 kcal)
- Morning Snack: Greek Yogurt with Honey and Walnuts (200 kcal)
- Lunch: Grilled Chicken with Veggie Salad (600 kcal)
- Afternoon Snack: Carrot Sticks with Hummus (150 kcal)
- Dinner: Baked Cod with Asparagus and Sweet Potato (626 kcal)
- Evening Snack: Handful of almonds (100 kcal)

Friday
- Breakfast: Egg White Omelet with Veggies (300 kcal)
- Morning Snack: Banana with Almond Butter (200 kcal)
- Lunch: Mediterranean Tuna Salad (600 kcal)

- Afternoon Snack: Grapes and Cheese (150 kcal)
- Dinner: Grilled Chicken with Ratatouille (450 kcal)
- Evening Snack: Greek Yogurt with Honey (100 kcal)

Saturday
- Breakfast: Greek Yogurt Parfait (250 kcal)
- Morning Snack: Handful of Almonds and a Banana (200 kcal)
- Lunch: Cod and Veggie Stir Fry (600 kcal)
- Afternoon Snack: Apple and Peanut Butter (150 kcal)
- Dinner: Grilled Tuna with Quinoa Salad (650 kcal)
- Evening Snack: Greek Yogurt with Honey (100 kcal)

Sunday
- Breakfast: Egg White Omelet with Veggies (300 kcal)
- Morning Snack: Banana with Almond Butter (200 kcal)
- Lunch: Greek Chicken Salad (600 kcal)
- Afternoon Snack: Carrot Sticks with Hummus (150 kcal)
- Dinner: Baked Salmon with Sweet Potato and Asparagus (626 kcal)
- Evening Snack: Handful of almonds (100 kcal)

Water intake: Minimum 2 liters per day.

Week 2

Monday
- **Breakfast**: Strawberry Banana Smoothie (250 kcal)
- **Morning Snack**: Cottage Cheese with Peach (100 kcal)
- **Lunch**: Grilled Beef Salad with Avocado (600 kcal)
- **Afternoon Snack**: Cherry Tomatoes and Mozzarella Skewers (150 kcal)
- **Dinner**: Lemon Herb Baked Cod with Broccoli and Sweet Potatoes (700 kcal)
- **Evening Snack**: Blueberries and Greek Yogurt (200 kcal)

Tuesday
- **Breakfast**: Protein Pancakes with Blueberries (250 kcal)
- **Morning Snack**: Hard-Boiled Egg with a slice of Grana Padano (150 kcal)
- **Lunch**: Quinoa and Tuna Salad (600 kcal)
- **Afternoon Snack**: Apple and Almond Butter (200 kcal)

- **Dinner**: Grilled Turkey with Steamed Vegetables (700 kcal)
- **Evening Snack**: Handful of Mixed Nuts (100 kcal)

Wednesday
- **Breakfast**: Greek Yogurt with Mixed Berries and Almonds (250 kcal)
- **Morning Snack**: Grapes and a Slice of Grana Padano (150 kcal)
- **Lunch**: Baked Salmon with Brown Rice and Asparagus (700 kcal)
- **Afternoon Snack**: Carrot and Cucumber Sticks with Hummus (100 kcal)
- **Dinner**: Chicken Stir Fry with Bell Peppers and Mushrooms (600 kcal)
- **Evening Snack**: Greek Yogurt with Honey (200 kcal)

Thursday
- **Breakfast**: Scrambled Egg Whites with Spinach and Tomatoes (250 kcal)
- **Morning Snack**: Banana and Almond Butter (150 kcal)
- **Lunch**: Grilled Chicken and Avocado Salad (600 kcal)
- **Afternoon Snack**: Cottage Cheese with Pineapple (100 kcal)
- **Dinner**: Grilled Sardines with Steamed Broccoli and Quinoa (700 kcal)
- **Evening Snack**: Handful of Mixed Berries (200 kcal)

Friday
- **Breakfast**: Oatmeal with Cinnamon and Apple (250 kcal)
- **Morning Snack**: Hard-Boiled Egg with a slice of Grana Padano (150 kcal)
- **Lunch**: Tuna and Mixed Bean Salad (600 kcal)
- **Afternoon Snack**: Greek Yogurt with Sliced Kiwi (100 kcal)
- **Dinner**: Baked Turkey with Sweet Potato and Green Beans (700 kcal)
- **Evening Snack**: Handful of Almonds (200 kcal)

Saturday
- **Breakfast**: Protein Smoothie with Spinach and Banana (250 kcal)
- **Morning Snack**: Cottage Cheese with Blueberries (150 kcal)
- **Lunch**: Baked Cod with Brown Rice and Steamed Asparagus (700 kcal)
- **Afternoon Snack**: Carrot and Cucumber Sticks with Hummus (100 kcal)

- **Dinner**: Grilled Chicken with Quinoa and Roasted Brussels Sprouts (600 kcal)
- **Evening Snack**: Greek Yogurt with Honey (200 kcal)

Sunday
- **Breakfast**: Scrambled Eggs with Avocado and Salsa (300 kcal)
- **Morning Snack**: Apple and Almond Butter (150 kcal)
- **Lunch**: Turkey and Mixed Bean Salad (600 kcal)
- **Afternoon Snack**: Cottage Cheese with Peach (100 kcal)
- **Dinner**: Baked Salmon with Sweet Potato and Steamed Broccoli (700 kcal)
- **Evening Snack**: Handful of Mixed Nuts (150 kcal)

Week 3

Monday
- **Breakfast**: Almond Milk Oatmeal with Berries (250 kcal)
- **Morning Snack**: Greek Yogurt with Honey (150 kcal)
- **Lunch**: Grilled Sardines with Quinoa and Broccoli (700 kcal)
- **Afternoon Snack**: Apple and a Slice of Grana Padano (150 kcal)
- **Dinner**: Chicken Stir Fry with Bell Peppers and Mushrooms (600 kcal)
- **Evening Snack**: Cottage Cheese with Peach (150 kcal)

Tuesday
- **Breakfast**: Banana and Blueberry Protein Smoothie (250 kcal)
- **Morning Snack**: Handful of Almonds (150 kcal)
- **Lunch**: Baked Cod with Brown Rice and Asparagus (700 kcal)
- **Afternoon Snack**: Carrot and Cucumber Sticks with Hummus (100 kcal)
- **Dinner**: Grilled Turkey with Steamed Vegetables (700 kcal)
- **Evening Snack**: Greek Yogurt with Mixed Berries (100 kcal)

Wednesday
- **Breakfast**: Scrambled Eggs with Avocado and Tomatoes (250 kcal)

- **Morning Snack**: Hard-Boiled Egg with a slice of Grana Padano (150 kcal)
- **Lunch**: Grilled Chicken and Avocado Salad (600 kcal)
- **Afternoon Snack**: Greek Yogurt with Sliced Kiwi (150 kcal)
- **Dinner**: Lemon Herb Baked Cod with Broccoli and Sweet Potatoes (700 kcal)
- **Evening Snack**: Handful of Mixed Berries (150 kcal)

Thursday
- **Breakfast**: Protein Pancakes with Blueberries (250 kcal)
- **Morning Snack**: Banana and Almond Butter (150 kcal)
- **Lunch**: Tuna and Mixed Bean Salad (600 kcal)
- **Afternoon Snack**: Cottage Cheese with Pineapple (150 kcal)
- **Dinner**: Baked Turkey with Sweet Potato and Green Beans (700 kcal)
- **Evening Snack**: Handful of Mixed Nuts (150 kcal)

Friday
- **Breakfast**: Greek Yogurt with Mixed Berries and Almonds (250 kcal)
- **Morning Snack**: Grapes and a Slice of Grana Padano (150 kcal)
- **Lunch**: Baked Salmon with Brown Rice and Asparagus (700 kcal)
- **Afternoon Snack**: Carrot and Cucumber Sticks with Hummus (100 kcal)
- **Dinner**: Grilled Beef Salad with Avocado (600 kcal)
- **Evening Snack**: Greek Yogurt with Honey (200 kcal)

Saturday
- **Breakfast**: Scrambled Egg Whites with Spinach and Tomatoes (250 kcal)
- **Morning Snack**: Cottage Cheese with Blueberries (150 kcal)
- **Lunch**: Quinoa and Tuna Salad (600 kcal)
- **Afternoon Snack**: Apple and Almond Butter (200 kcal)
- **Dinner**: Grilled Turkey with Steamed Vegetables (700 kcal)
- **Evening Snack**: Handful of Almonds (100 kcal)

Sunday
- **Breakfast**: Oatmeal with Cinnamon and Apple (250 kcal)
- **Morning Snack**: Hard-Boiled Egg with a slice of Grana Padano (150 kcal)
- **Lunch**: Turkey and Mixed Bean Salad (600 kcal)

- **Afternoon Snack**: Cherry Tomatoes and Mozzarella Skewers (150 kcal)
- **Dinner**: Baked Salmon with Sweet Potato and Steamed Broccoli (700 kcal)
- **Evening Snack**: Greek Yogurt with Honey (150 kcal)

Week 4

Monday
- **Breakfast**: Overnight Chia Pudding with Mixed Berries (250 kcal)
- **Morning Snack**: Cottage Cheese with Sliced Pear (150 kcal)
- **Lunch**: Quinoa Salad with Grilled Vegetables and Tuna (600 kcal)
- **Afternoon Snack**: Greek Yogurt with Honey (150 kcal)
- **Dinner**: Baked Cod with Steamed Green Beans and Rice (700 kcal)
- **Evening Snack**: Slice of Grana Padano with a Handful of Walnuts (150 kcal)

Tuesday
- **Breakfast**: Greek Yogurt with Banana and Almond Butter (250 kcal)
- **Morning Snack**: Apple and a Slice of Grana Padano (150 kcal)
- **Lunch**: Baked Chicken Breast with Quinoa and Broccoli (700 kcal)
- **Afternoon Snack**: Handful of Mixed Nuts (200 kcal)
- **Dinner**: Grilled Turkey Salad with Avocado (600 kcal)
- **Evening Snack**: Greek Yogurt with Mixed Berries (100 kcal)

Wednesday
- **Breakfast**: Protein Smoothie with Banana and Blueberries (250 kcal)
- **Morning Snack**: Carrot and Cucumber Sticks with Hummus (100 kcal)
- **Lunch**: Grilled Sardines with Brown Rice and Asparagus (700 kcal)
- **Afternoon Snack**: Greek Yogurt with Sliced Kiwi (150 kcal)

- **Dinner**: Lemon Herb Baked Salmon with Sweet Potatoes (700 kcal)
- **Evening Snack**: Hard-Boiled Egg (150 kcal)

Thursday
- **Breakfast**: Scrambled Eggs with Avocado and Tomatoes (250 kcal)
- **Morning Snack**: Cottage Cheese with Pineapple (150 kcal)
- **Lunch**: Turkey and Mixed Bean Salad (600 kcal)
- **Afternoon Snack**: Handful of Almonds (150 kcal)
- **Dinner**: Grilled Chicken Breast with Steamed Vegetables (700 kcal)
- **Evening Snack**: Greek Yogurt with Honey (150 kcal)

Friday
- **Breakfast**: Oatmeal with Almond Milk and Berries (250 kcal)
- **Morning Snack**: Banana and a Slice of Grana Padano (150 kcal)
- **Lunch**: Baked Cod with Quinoa and Broccoli (700 kcal)
- **Afternoon Snack**: Carrot and Cucumber Sticks with Hummus (100 kcal)
- **Dinner**: Beef Stir Fry with Bell Peppers and Mushrooms (700 kcal)
- **Evening Snack**: Cottage Cheese with Peach (100 kcal)

Saturday
- **Breakfast**: Greek Yogurt with Mixed Berries and Almonds (250 kcal)
- **Morning Snack**: Apple with Almond Butter (150 kcal)
- **Lunch**: Grilled Turkey and Avocado Salad (600 kcal)
- **Afternoon Snack**: Cherry Tomatoes and Mozzarella Skewers (200 kcal)
- **Dinner**: Lemon Herb Baked Salmon with Steamed Broccoli (700 kcal)
- **Evening Snack**: Greek Yogurt with Honey (100 kcal)

Sunday
- **Breakfast**: Protein Pancakes with Blueberries (250 kcal)
- **Morning Snack**: Hard-Boiled Egg with a Slice of Grana Padano (150 kcal)
- **Lunch**: Baked Chicken Breast with Sweet Potato and Green Beans (700 kcal)
- **Afternoon Snack**: Greek Yogurt with Sliced Kiwi (150 kcal)

- **Dinner**: Grilled Beef Salad with Avocado (600 kcal)
- **Evening Snack**: Handful of Mixed Nuts (150 kcal)

Week 5:

Monday
- **Breakfast:** Quinoa Porridge with Mixed Berries and Nuts (320 Kcal)
- **Snack 1:** Baked Apple with Cinnamon and Almonds (200 Kcal)
- **Lunch:** Whole Wheat Pasta with Spinach and Salmon (650 Kcal)
- **Snack 2:** 2 Rice Cakes with Hummus (100 Kcal)
- **Dinner:** Baked Cod with Quinoa and Steamed Vegetables (700 Kcal)
- **After-Dinner Snack:** Sliced Banana with a Dollop of Greek Yogurt (30 Kcal)

Tuesday
- **Breakfast:** Greek Yogurt with Mixed Berries and Granola (300 Kcal)
- **Snack 1:** Handful of Nuts and Seeds (200 Kcal)
- **Lunch:** Chicken Caesar Salad with Whole Grain Croutons (650 Kcal)
- **Snack 2:** Sliced Cucumber with 2 tbsp. Cream Cheese (100 Kcal)
- **Dinner:** Beef Stir Fry with Brown Rice (700 Kcal)
- **After-Dinner Snack:** A Small Pear (50 Kcal)

Wednesday
- **Breakfast:** Whole Grain Toast with Avocado and Poached Eggs (350 Kcal)
- **Snack 1:** Sliced Pear with Grana Padano Cheese (200 Kcal)
- **Lunch:** Tuna and Veggie Stuffed Bell Peppers (700 Kcal)
- **Snack 2:** Carrot and Celery Sticks with 2 tbsp. Peanut Butter (150 Kcal)
- **Dinner:** Turkey and Quinoa Stuffed Eggplant (650 Kcal)
- **After-Dinner Snack:** A Handful of Blueberries (50 Kcal)

Thursday
- **Breakfast:** Banana Pancakes with a Drizzle of Honey (300 Kcal)
- **Snack 1:** Sliced Apple with Almond Butter (200 Kcal)
- **Lunch:** Zucchini Noodles with Shrimp and Cherry Tomatoes (700 Kcal)
- **Snack 2:** Greek Yogurt with a Handful of Blueberries (100 Kcal)
- **Dinner:** Baked Chicken Thigh with Couscous and Steamed Vegetables (700 Kcal)
- **After-Dinner Snack:** A Small Apple (50 Kcal)

Friday
- **Breakfast:** Whole Grain Cereal with Skim Milk and Sliced Banana (300 Kcal)
- **Snack 1:** Cherry Tomatoes with Mozzarella Cheese (200 Kcal)
- **Lunch:** Roasted Salmon with Sweet Potato and Green Beans (700 Kcal)
- **Snack 2:** Orange and a Handful of Almonds (100 Kcal)
- **Dinner:** Quinoa Salad with Grilled Chicken, Avocado, and Black Beans (700 Kcal)
- **After-Dinner Snack:** A Few Slices of Kiwi (50 Kcal)

Saturday
- **Breakfast:** Scrambled Eggs with Spinach and Feta Cheese (350 Kcal)
- **Snack 1:** Sliced Melon with Grana Padano Cheese (200 Kcal)
- **Lunch:** Grilled Tuna Steak with Asparagus and Brown Rice (650 Kcal)
- **Snack 2:** Celery Sticks with 2 tbsp. Hummus (100 Kcal)
- **Dinner:** Baked Turkey Meatballs with Whole Wheat Spaghetti and Tomato Sauce (700 Kcal)
- **After-Dinner Snack:** A Small Orange (50 Kcal)

Sunday
- **Breakfast:** Smoothie Bowl with Mixed Berries, Banana, and Chia Seeds (300 Kcal)
- **Snack 1:** A Handful of Mixed Nuts (200 Kcal)
- **Lunch:** Chicken and Veggie Stir Fry with Quinoa (700 Kcal)
- **Snack 2:** Sliced Peach with Cottage Cheese (100 Kcal)

- **Dinner:** Baked Cod with a Side of Steamed Broccoli and Sweet Potato (700 Kcal)
- **After-Dinner Snack:** A Few Strawberries (50 Kcal)

Week 6:

Monday
- **Breakfast:** Oatmeal with Almonds and Honey (300 Kcal)
- **Snack 1:** A Handful of Mixed Berries (100 Kcal)
- **Lunch:** Veggie Stir Fry with Tofu and Brown Rice (700 Kcal)
- **Snack 2:** Carrot Sticks with Hummus (100 Kcal)
- **Dinner:** Grilled Chicken Breast with Steamed Vegetables and Quinoa (700 Kcal)
- **After-Dinner Snack:** Greek Yogurt with a drizzle of Honey (100 Kcal)

Tuesday
- **Breakfast:** Whole Grain Toast with Avocado and Scrambled Eggs (350 Kcal)
- **Snack 1:** Banana with Almond Butter (150 Kcal)
- **Lunch:** Whole Wheat Pasta with Shrimp and Cherry Tomatoes (650 Kcal)
- **Snack 2:** A Handful of Almonds (100 Kcal)
- **Dinner:** Turkey and Veggie Stuffed Bell Peppers (700 Kcal)
- **After-Dinner Snack:** Cottage Cheese with Sliced Peaches (50 Kcal)

Wednesday
- **Breakfast:** Greek Yogurt with Granola and Mixed Berries (300 Kcal)
- **Snack 1:** Sliced Cucumber and Cherry Tomatoes (100 Kcal)
- **Lunch:** Baked Salmon with Sweet Potato and Asparagus (700 Kcal)
- **Snack 2:** A Small Apple (50 Kcal)
- **Dinner:** Beef Stir Fry with Quinoa and Vegetables (700 Kcal)
- **After-Dinner Snack:** A Handful of Blueberries (50 Kcal)

Thursday
- **Breakfast:** Quinoa Porridge with Honey and Nuts (350 Kcal)

- **Snack 1:** A Handful of Grapes (100 Kcal)
- **Lunch:** Chicken Caesar Salad with Whole Grain Croutons (700 Kcal)
- **Snack 2:** A Banana (100 Kcal)
- **Dinner:** Shrimp and Veggie Stuffed Eggplant (700 Kcal)
- **After-Dinner Snack:** Greek Yogurt with Sliced Strawberries (50 Kcal)

Friday
- **Breakfast:** Banana Pancakes with a drizzle of Honey (300 Kcal)
- **Snack 1:** Orange and a Handful of Almonds (200 Kcal)
- **Lunch:** Grilled Tuna Steak with Brown Rice and Steamed Vegetables (650 Kcal)
- **Snack 2:** Sliced Apple with Peanut Butter (150 Kcal)
- **Dinner:** Turkey Meatballs with Whole Wheat Pasta and Tomato Sauce (700 Kcal)
- **After-Dinner Snack:** A Few Slices of Kiwi (50 Kcal)

Saturday
- **Breakfast:** Scrambled Eggs with Spinach and Whole Grain Toast (350 Kcal)
- **Snack 1:** Sliced Melon with Grana Padano Cheese (200 Kcal)
- **Lunch:** Zucchini Noodles with Chicken and Cherry Tomatoes (700 Kcal)
- **Snack 2:** A Handful of Mixed Nuts and Seeds (150 Kcal)
- **Dinner:** Baked Cod with Couscous and Steamed Broccoli (700 Kcal)
- **After-Dinner Snack:** A Small Orange (50 Kcal)

Sunday
- **Breakfast:** Smoothie Bowl with Banana, Spinach, and Chia Seeds (300 Kcal)
- **Snack 1:** A Handful of Mixed Berries (100 Kcal)
- **Lunch:** Roasted Chicken with Sweet Potato and Green Beans (700 Kcal)
- **Snack 2:** Carrot and Celery Sticks with Hummus (100 Kcal)
- **Dinner:** Quinoa Salad with Grilled Shrimp, Avocado, and Black Beans (700 Kcal)
- **After-Dinner Snack:** Greek Yogurt with a Handful of Blueberries (100 Kcal)

Week 7:

Monday
- **Breakfast:** Overnight Chia Pudding with Almond Milk and Berries (300 Kcal)
- **Snack 1:** An Apple (80 Kcal)
- **Lunch:** Shrimp and Quinoa Salad with Mixed Greens (700 Kcal)
- **Snack 2:** Greek Yogurt with a Handful of Walnuts (200 Kcal)
- **Dinner:** Baked Cod with Lemon, Steamed Asparagus, and Brown Rice (700 Kcal)
- **After-Dinner Snack:** A Banana (120 Kcal)

Tuesday
- **Breakfast:** Scrambled Eggs with Spinach and Feta Cheese (350 Kcal)
- **Snack 1:** A Medium Orange (80 Kcal)
- **Lunch:** Chicken Caesar Salad (700 Kcal)
- **Snack 2:** Hummus with Carrot Sticks (100 Kcal)
- **Dinner:** Grilled Beef with Roasted Brussels Sprouts and Sweet Potatoes (700 Kcal)
- **After-Dinner Snack:** Greek Yogurt with a drizzle of Honey (50 Kcal)

Wednesday
- **Breakfast:** Greek Yogurt with Granola and Fresh Berries (300 Kcal)
- **Snack 1:** A Handful of Almonds (160 Kcal)
- **Lunch:** Tuna and Avocado Wrap (700 Kcal)
- **Snack 2:** A Pear (100 Kcal)
- **Dinner:** Grilled Salmon with Lemon, Steamed Broccoli, and Quinoa (700 Kcal)
- **After-Dinner Snack:** Dark Chocolate Square (60 Kcal)

Thursday
- **Breakfast:** Oatmeal with Banana and Honey (300 Kcal)
- **Snack 1:** A Medium Apple (80 Kcal)
- **Lunch:** Quinoa Salad with Roasted Vegetables and Grilled Chicken (700 Kcal)
- **Snack 2:** A Handful of Walnuts (200 Kcal)

- **Dinner:** Baked Turkey with Sweet Potato and Green Beans (700 Kcal)
- **After-Dinner Snack:** Greek Yogurt with a drizzle of Honey (50 Kcal)

Friday
- **Breakfast:** Whole Grain Toast with Almond Butter and Sliced Strawberries (300 Kcal)
- **Snack 1:** A Medium Orange (80 Kcal)
- **Lunch:** Shrimp Caesar Salad (700 Kcal)
- **Snack 2:** Greek Yogurt with a Spoonful of Chia Seeds (150 Kcal)
- **Dinner:** Grilled Beef with Roasted Brussels Sprouts and Sweet Potatoes (700 Kcal)
- **After-Dinner Snack:** Dark Chocolate Square (60 Kcal)

Saturday
- **Breakfast:** Scrambled Eggs with Avocado and Tomato on Whole Grain Bread (350 Kcal)
- **Snack 1:** A Medium Apple (80 Kcal)
- **Lunch:** Grilled Chicken with Steamed Vegetables and Brown Rice (700 Kcal)
- **Snack 2:** A Handful of Walnuts (200 Kcal)
- **Dinner:** Turkey and Vegetable Stir-Fry with Quinoa (650 Kcal)
- **After-Dinner Snack:** Greek Yogurt with a drizzle of Honey (50 Kcal)

Sunday
- **Breakfast:** Quinoa Porridge with Almonds and Berries (350 Kcal)
- **Snack 1:** Sliced Cucumber with Hummus (100 Kcal)
- **Lunch:** Baked Tuna Steak with Brown Rice and Steamed Vegetables (700 Kcal)
- **Snack 2:** A Handful of Mixed Berries (100 Kcal)
- **Dinner:** Beef Stir Fry with Quinoa and Mixed Vegetables (700 Kcal)
- **After-Dinner Snack:** A Banana (120 Kcal)

Week 8

- **Monday**

Breakfast: Wholemeal toast with almond butter and banana (300 Kcal)
- **Snack 1:** A medium pear (100 Kcal)
- **Lunch:** Brown rice with baked chicken and steamed vegetables (700 Kcal)
- **Snack 2:** A handful of almonds (150 Kcal)
- **Dinner:** Baked cod with sweet potatoes and green beans (700 Kcal)
- **After-dinner snack:** Greek yogurt with a drizzle of Honey (50 Kcal)

Tuesday
- **Breakfast:** Scrambled eggs with avocado and tomato with wholemeal bread (350 Kcal)
- **Snack 1**: A medium apple (80 Kcal)
- **Lunch:** Tuna salad with mixed vegetables and small tomatoes (700 Kcal)
- **Snack 2:** A handful of walnuts (200 Kcal)
- **Dinner:** Turkey and sautéed vegetables with quinoa (650 Kcal)
- **After-dinner snack:** A small orange (80 Kcal)

Wednesday
- **Breakfast:** Quinoa Porridge with Almonds and Berries (350 Kcal)
- **Snack 1:** Sliced Cucumber with Hummus (100 Kcal)
- **Lunch:** Whole Grain Pasta with Grilled Shrimp and Bell Peppers (700 Kcal)
- **Snack 2:** Greek Yogurt with a Spoonful of Chia Seeds (150 Kcal)
- **Dinner:** Baked Salmon with Steamed Asparagus and Brown Rice (650 Kcal)
- **After-Dinner Snack:** A Handful of Blueberries (60 Kcal)

Thursday
- **Breakfast:** Oatmeal with Banana and Honey (300 Kcal)
- **Snack 1:** A Medium Pear (100 Kcal)

- **Lunch:** Grilled Chicken Caesar Salad (700 Kcal)
- **Snack 2:** A Handful of Almonds (150 Kcal)
- **Dinner:** Baked Cod with Sweet Potato and Green Beans (700 Kcal)
- **After-Dinner Snack:** A Banana (100 Kcal)

Friday

- **Breakfast:** Warmed wholemeal bread with almond butter and sliced strawberries (300 Kcal)
- **Snack 1:** A handful of grapes (100 Kcal)
- **Lunch:** Tuna salad with various vegetables and small tomatoes (700 Kcal)
- **Snack 2:** Sliced cucumber with hummus (100 Kcal)
- **Dinner:** Grilled beef with steamed broccoli and quinoa (700 Kcal)
- **After-dinner snack:** Greek yoghurt with a drizzle of honey (50 Kcal)

Saturday
- **Breakfast:** Scrambled Eggs with Avocado and Tomato on Whole Grain Bread (350 Kcal)
- **Snack 1:** A Medium Apple (80 Kcal)
- **Lunch:** Whole Wheat Pasta with Shrimp and Broccoli (700 Kcal)
- **Snack 2:** A Handful of Walnuts (200 Kcal)
- **Dinner:** Turkey and Vegetable Stir-Fry with Quinoa (650 Kcal)
- **After-Dinner Snack:** A Small Orange (80 Kcal)

Sunday
- **Breakfast:** White yoghurt with granola and mixed berries (300 Kcal)
- **Snack 1:** One banana with peanut butter (200 Kcal)
- **Lunch:** Baked tuna steak with brown rice and steamed vegetables (700 Kcal)
- **Snack 2:** A handful of mixed berries (100 Kcal)
- **Dinner:** Stir-fried beef with quinoa and mixed vegetables (700 Kcal)
- **After-dinner snack:** A handful of blueberries (50 Kcal)

To drink at least 2 litres of water a day!

Monday
- **Breakfast:** Whole grain waffles with Greek yogurt, blueberries, and a drizzle of honey (350 Kcal)
- **Snack 1:** Sliced cucumber and bell peppers with tzatziki (100 Kcal)
- **Lunch:** Lemon herb grilled chicken breast with a side of roasted zucchini and cherry tomatoes (700 Kcal)
- **Snack 2:** Fresh figs (100 Kcal)
- **Dinner:** Eggplant, spinach, and ricotta stuffed cannelloni with a side salad (700 Kcal)
- **After-Dinner Snack:** Dark chocolate-covered almonds (50 Kcal)

Tuesday
- **Breakfast:** Omelette with mushrooms, spinach, and feta cheese (350 Kcal)
- **Snack 1:** Apple slices with a tablespoon of almond butter (150 Kcal)
- **Lunch:** Lentil and vegetable stew with a slice of whole grain bread (700 Kcal)
- **Snack 2:** Kiwi fruit (80 Kcal)
- **Dinner:** Pan-seared tilapia with sautéed green beans and quinoa (700 Kcal)
- **After-Dinner Snack:** Greek yogurt with a sprinkle of flaxseeds (20 Kcal)

Wednesday
- **Breakfast:** Overnight oats with chia seeds, mango, and coconut flakes (320 Kcal)
- **Snack 1:** Dried apricots (80 Kcal)
- **Lunch:** Chickpea salad with olives, cherry tomatoes, feta, and a lemon-oregano dressing (700 Kcal)
- **Snack 2:** Carrot sticks with hummus (100 Kcal)
- **Dinner:** Spaghetti with cherry tomatoes, garlic, chili flakes, and arugula (700 Kcal)
- **After-Dinner Snack:** Handful of walnuts (100 Kcal)

Thursday

- **Breakfast:** Toast with wholemeal bread with avocado and poached egg (350 Kcal)
- **Snack 1:** Fresh pineapple pieces (100 Kcal)
- **Lunch:** Chicken breast stuffed with spinach and cottage cheese with a side of steamed broccoli (700 Kcal)
- **Snack 2:** Ricotta cheese with a sprinkling of sunflower seeds (150 Kcal)
- **Dinner:** Stir-fried tofu with mixed vegetables and brown rice (700 Kcal)
- **After-dinner snack:** A cup of camomile tea with a teaspoon of honey (20 Kcal)

Friday
- **Breakfast:** Fruit salad with strawberries, melon, and grapes topped with Greek yogurt (300 Kcal)
- **Snack 1:** Handful of roasted chickpeas (100 Kcal)
- **Lunch:** Beef and vegetable kebabs with a side of tabbouleh (700 Kcal)
- **Snack 2:** Freshly squeezed orange juice (110 Kcal)
- **Dinner:** Zucchini noodles with pesto and cherry tomatoes (690 Kcal)
- **After-Dinner Snack:** Dark chocolate square (70 Kcal)

Saturday
- **Breakfast:** Pancakes with maple syrup, raspberries and a little cottage cheese (350 Kcal)
- **Snack 1:** Mixed nuts (150 Kcal)
- **Lunch:** Turkey meat and low-fat cheese with a side salad (700 Kcal)
- **Snack 2:** Greek yoghurt with a handful of muesli (150 Kcal)
- **Dinner:** Grilled salmon with lemon, asparagus and couscous salad (700 Kcal)
- **After-dinner snack:** Fresh berries (50 Kcal)

Sunday
- **Breakfast:** Scrambled eggs with smoked salmon on a bed of spinach (340 Kcal)
- **Snack 1:** Sliced pear (80 Kcal)
- **Lunch:** Vegetable lasagna with a side of mixed greens (700 Kcal)
- **Snack 2:** Rice cakes with almond butter (180 Kcal)

- **Dinner:** Lamb chops with mint sauce, sautéed Brussels sprouts, and roasted potatoes (700 Kcal)
- **After-Dinner Snack:** A cup of green tea and two date energy balls (80 Kcal)

Week 10

Monday
- **Breakfast:** Smoothie bowl made with banana, spinach, almond milk, topped with granola and pumpkin seeds (350 Kcal)
- **Snack 1:** Handful of roasted seaweed snack (50 Kcal)
- **Lunch:** Cauliflower rice stir-fried with shrimp, bell peppers, and snap peas (700 Kcal)
- **Snack 2:** Cherry tomatoes with mozzarella balls (100 Kcal)
- **Dinner:** Grilled steak with a side of sweet potato wedges and steamed green beans (700 Kcal)
- **After-Dinner Snack:** Herbal tea and dark chocolate (100 Kcal)

Tuesday
- **Breakfast:** Whole grain porridge with blueberries, almonds, and a drizzle of honey (340 Kcal)
- **Snack 1:** Fresh orange segments (60 Kcal)
- **Lunch:** Quinoa salad with roasted beetroot, goat cheese, walnuts, and a balsamic glaze (700 Kcal)
- **Snack 2:** Sliced cucumber with a hummus dip (90 Kcal)
- **Dinner:** Chicken tikka masala with brown rice (700 Kcal)
- **After-Dinner Snack:** Two whole wheat crackers with cheese (110 Kcal)

Wednesday
- **Breakfast:** Muesli with Greek yogurt, sliced strawberries, and a sprinkling of chia seeds (330 Kcal)
- **Snack 1:** Carrot sticks with tzatziki (70 Kcal)
- **Lunch:** Lentil soup with a wholemeal sandwich (700 Kcal)
- **Snack 2:** Small bowl of mixed berries (80 Kcal)
- **Dinner:** Vegetable curry with chickpeas and a side of wholemeal couscous (700 Kcal)

- **After-dinner snack:** Warm almond milk with a pinch of turmeric and honey (120 Kcal)

Thursday
- **Breakfast:** Scrambled tofu with tomatoes, onions, and spinach on whole grain toast (340 Kcal)
- **Snack 1:** Dried figs (70 Kcal)
- **Lunch:** Spinach and feta stuffed peppers with a side salad (700 Kcal)
- **Snack 2:** Greek yogurt with sliced kiwi (100 Kcal)
- **Dinner:** Baked trout with lemon and herbs, steamed asparagus, and quinoa (700 Kcal)
- **After-Dinner Snack:** A small apple and a piece of cheese (90 Kcal)

Friday
- **Breakfast:** Banana and nut butter smoothie with a scoop of protein powder (350 Kcal)
- **Snack 1:** Handful of pistachios (80 Kcal)
- **Lunch:** Whole grain wrap with turkey, lettuce, tomato, and light mayo (700 Kcal)
- **Snack 2:** Cottage cheese with pineapple chunks (100 Kcal)
- **Dinner:** Vegetable paella with saffron and olives (700 Kcal)
- **After-Dinner Snack:** Chamomile tea and a slice of whole grain toast with jam (70 Kcal)

Saturday
-
- **Breakfast:** French bread with maple syrup and a side of mixed fruit (360 Kcal)
- **Snack 1:** two oatmeal biscuits (80 Kcal)
- **Lunch:** Tomato and mozzarella caprese salad with basil and balsamic reduction (700 Kcal)
- **Snack 2:** Handful of mixed nuts (120 Kcal)
- **Dinner:** Roast pork loin with apple sauce, green beans and mashed potatoes (700 Kcal)
- **After-dinner snack:** A square of dark chocolate and a small pear (50 Kcal)

Sunday
- **Breakfast:** Whole grain pancakes with raspberry compote (340 Kcal)
- **Snack 1:** Freshly squeezed grapefruit juice (60 Kcal)
- **Lunch:** Butternut squash and sage risotto (700 Kcal)

- **Snack 2:** Sliced bell peppers with guacamole (100 Kcal)
- **Dinner:** Grilled lamb koftas with tzatziki and a tabbouleh salad (700 Kcal)
- **After-Dinner Snack:** Two digestive biscuits with a cup of green tea (120 Kcal)

Week 11

Monday
- **Breakfast:** Chia seed pudding topped with mango slices and coconut flakes (340 Kcal)
- **Snack 1:** Celery sticks with a light cream cheese dip (50 Kcal)
- **Lunch:** Chickpea salad with cherry tomatoes, cucumbers, red onions, feta, and a lemon dressing (700 Kcal)
- **Snack 2:** Hard-boiled egg sprinkled with a pinch of salt and pepper (70 Kcal)
- **Dinner:** Grilled sea bass with a side of roasted broccoli and garlic butter (690 Kcal)
- **After-Dinner Snack:** Rooibos tea and a square of 80% dark chocolate (150 Kcal)

Tuesday
- **Breakfast:** Whole grain waffle with cottage cheese and blackberry compote (330 Kcal)
- **Snack 1:** Edamame beans sprinkled with sea salt (60 Kcal)
- **Lunch:** Beef stir-fry with snap peas, bell peppers, and a teriyaki sauce served over brown rice (700 Kcal)
- **Snack 2:** A small bowl of mixed fruit salad (90 Kcal)
- **Dinner:** Spaghetti squash with homemade tomato basil sauce and parmesan cheese (690 Kcal)
- **After-Dinner Snack:** Herbal tea with a rice cake topped with almond butter (130 Kcal)

Wednesday
- **Breakfast:** Poached eggs on avocado toast with red chili flakes (340 Kcal)
- **Snack 1:** A slice of cantaloupe melon (50 Kcal)
- **Lunch:** Chicken Caesar salad with whole grain croutons and a light dressing (700 Kcal)

- **Snack 2:** A handful of roasted chickpeas (100 Kcal)
- **Dinner:** Zucchini noodles (zoodles) with a pesto and cherry tomato sauté (690 Kcal)
- **After-Dinner Snack:** Warm milk with honey and a sprinkle of cinnamon (120 Kcal)

Thursday
- **Breakfast:** Quinoa porridge with dried apricots, walnuts, and maple syrup (330 Kcal)
- **Snack 1:** A handful of blueberries (50 Kcal)
- Lunch: Moroccan lentil (400 gr) with a side of wholemeal pita bread (700 Kcal) -
- **Snack 2:** Greek yogurt with a drizzle of honey (100 Kcal)
- **Dinner:** Herb-crusted cod fillet with a side of mashed cauliflower and steamed spinach (690 Kcal)
- **After-Dinner Snack:** Chamomile tea and two almond biscotti (130 Kcal)

Friday
- **Breakfast:** Ricotta pancakes topped with fig slices and a hint of lemon zest (350 Kcal)
- **Snack 1:** A kiwi fruit (50 Kcal)
- **Lunch:** Beef and vegetable skewers with a side of bulgur wheat salad (700 Kcal)
- **Snack 2:** A small handful of olives (60 Kcal)
- **Dinner:** Vegetable and tofu green curry with basmati rice (700 Kcal)
- **After-Dinner Snack:** A glass of kefir with a teaspoon of flaxseeds (140 Kcal)

Saturday
- **Breakfast:** Frittata with mushrooms, spinach, and cherry tomatoes (340 Kcal)
- **Snack 1:** A small bunch of red grapes (60 Kcal)
- **Lunch:** Grilled chicken wrap with tzatziki, lettuce, and roasted red peppers (700 Kcal)
- **Snack 2:** A wedge of watermelon (70 Kcal)
- **Dinner:** Risotto with shrimp and asparagus (690 Kcal)
- **After-Dinner Snack:** Green tea with a slice of spelled toast and honey (140 Kcal)

Sunday

- **Breakfast:** Millet bowl with almond milk, sliced banana, and sunflower seeds (330 Kcal)
- **Snack 1:** Two tangerines (80 Kcal)
- **Lunch:** Turkey and cranberry sandwich on whole grain bread with a side salad (700 Kcal)
- **Snack 2:** Sliced radishes with a sprinkle of sea salt (30 Kcal)
- **Dinner:** Eggplant Parmesan with a side of mixed greens (700 Kcal)
- **After-Dinner Snack:** Rooibos tea and a homemade oatmeal cookie (160 Kcal)

Monday
- **Breakfast:** Amaranth porridge with sliced strawberries, chia seeds, and a dash of honey (320 Kcal)
- **Snack 1:** Carrot sticks with hummus dip (70 Kcal)
- **Lunch:** Grilled tempeh salad with arugula, beetroot, goat cheese, and a balsamic glaze (710 Kcal)
- **Snack 2:** A small bowl of papaya chunks (80 Kcal)
- **Dinner:** Lemon herb roasted chicken thighs with steamed green beans and quinoa (680 Kcal)
- **After-Dinner Snack:** Peppermint tea and a slice of whole grain bread with a thin layer of marmalade (140 Kcal)

Tuesday
- **Breakfast:** Muesli with skim milk, raisins, and almonds (340 Kcal)
- **Snack 1:** A small apple (80 Kcal)
- **Lunch:** Spinach and ricotta stuffed bell peppers with a side of wild rice (690 Kcal)
- **Snack 2:** A small handful of roasted sunflower seeds (90 Kcal)
- **Dinner:** Tuna steak with a ginger-soy glaze, served with bok choy and jasmine rice (700 Kcal)
- **After-Dinner Snack:** Decaf green tea and a couple of dried figs (100 Kcal)

Wednesday
- **Breakfast:** Rye toast with smoked salmon, cream cheese, and capers (340 Kcal)
- **Snack 1:** A pear (100 Kcal)
- **Lunch:** Tomato and red lentil soup with a slice of multigrain bread (680 Kcal)
- **Snack 2:** A handful of blueberries and a piece of cheddar cheese (130 Kcal)
- **Dinner:** Lamb chops with a mint sauce, sautéed kale, and roasted sweet potatoes (720 Kcal)
- **After-Dinner Snack:** Herbal tea and dark chocolate-covered almonds (30 Kcal)

Thursday
- **Breakfast:** Oat bran with kiwi slices, walnuts, and a dollop of Greek yogurt (320 Kcal)
- **Snack 1:** Cucumber slices with tzatziki (70 Kcal)
- **Lunch:** Black bean and corn salad with cilantro, cherry tomatoes, avocado, and a lime dressing (700 Kcal)
- **Snack 2:** Two plums (80 Kcal)
- **Dinner:** Grilled trout with a dill sauce, steamed asparagus, and pearl barley (700 Kcal)
- **After-Dinner Snack:** Warm almond milk with a touch of vanilla (130 Kcal)

Friday
- **Breakfast:** Crepes with wholemeal flour filled with berries and a sprinkling of icing sugar (350 Kcal)
- **Snack 1:** A slice of prosciutto wrapped around melon slices (80 Kcal)
- **Lunch:** Grilled portobello mushrooms topped with gorgonzola cheese, served with a salad of mixed vegetables (680 Kcal)
- **Snack 2:** A tangerine (60 Kcal)
- **Dinner:** Beef stew with carrots, potatoes, green peas and herbs (690 Kcal)
- **After-dinner snack:** Chamomile tea and a slice of rye bread with honey (140 Kcal)

Saturday
- **Breakfast:** Shakshuka with poached eggs in a spicy tomato sauce, sprinkled with feta (320 Kcal)
- **Snack 1:** Sliced radish with a sprinkle of sea salt (30 Kcal)
- **Lunch:** Grilled halloumi cheese salad with rocket, olives, and sundried tomatoes (690 Kcal)
- **Snack 2:** A small bowl of cherries (90 Kcal)
- **Dinner:** Turkey meatballs in a basil-tomato sauce, served with spaghetti squash (700 Kcal)
- **After-Dinner Snack:** A glass of kefir sprinkled with cocoa powder (170 Kcal)

Sunday
- **Breakfast:** Scrambled eggs with sautéed spinach, cherry tomatoes, and crumbled feta (320 Kcal)

- **Snack 1:** A small apricot (40 Kcal)
- **Lunch:** Roast beef with horseradish cream, green beans almandine, and mashed cauliflower (710 Kcal)
- **Snack 2:** Greek yogurt topped with pomegranate seeds (110 Kcal)
- **Dinner:** Vegetable curry with chickpeas, eggplant, zucchini, and served over basmati rice (700 Kcal)
- **After-Dinner Snack:** Licorice root tea with a couple of date rolls (130 Kcal)

Printed in Great Britain
by Amazon

40784352R00069